PRESENTED TO:

Mary Bell Miller

FROM:

Mary Bell Miller

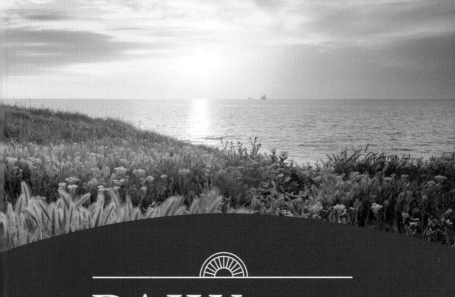

DAILY *in His* PRESENCE

DAVID JEREMIAH

Turning point

with Dr. David Jeremiah

with Dr. David Jeremiah

www.DavidJeremiah.org

Special thanks to William Kruidenier and Robert J. Morgan
Managing Editor: Myrna Davis

Printed in China.

For this reason I bow my knees to the Father of our Lord Jesus Christ, from whom the whole family in heaven and earth is named, that He would grant you, according to the riches of His glory, to be strengthened with might through His Spirit in the inner man, that Christ may dwell in your hearts through faith; that you, being rooted and grounded in love, may be able to comprehend with all the saints what is the width and length and depth and height—to know the love of Christ which passes knowledge; that you may be filled will all the fullness of God.

EPHESIANS 3:14-19

INTRODUCTION

Daily in His Presence—
Developing 20/20 Vision

The joy of seeing clearly is something people often take for granted. If your vision is 20/20, you are blessed. Some children discover early in their education that they can't see the instructions on the white board clearly and that they need to wear glasses. Others find the need for "corrected vision" in their twenties, and then many of us have discovered as we get older that we cannot read the small print on a prescription bottle or other small print without the aid of "readers." The frustration of not seeing something clearly is real, but with innovative surgical procedures and improved contacts, many people no longer wear glasses and enjoy seeing clearly.

Having 20/20 vision is something many people have never experienced in this life but developing a clear vision for God and His Word is available to each one of us. We can know God better. We can see Him more clearly. We can understand His will for us. How does this happen? By seeking His face and His Word daily. By setting aside a time for God and getting to know Him better—by making Him a priority. When making a choice about how to spend our time, we need to choose wisely, we need to have our sights set beyond this world and choose to know God better.

It is our sincere prayer that with this 366-day devotional, you will take the time each day to draw closer to God. As you seek to know Him better, you will discover an awareness of His presence throughout the day—in your thoughts, in your actions, and even your speech. Improve your 20/20 vision for God by spending time *Daily in His Presence*.

JANUARY

JANUARY 1
A Powerhouse of Promises

His divine power has given to us all things that pertain to life and godliness, through the knowledge of Him who called us by glory and virtue, by which have been given to us exceedingly great and precious promises.

2 PETER 1:3-4

Hundreds of promises are given in Scripture to believers who choose to live in obedience to God's Word. This heavenly bank of promises is powerful and purposeful for *all* our needs. When God provides for us, He gives lavishly from His riches. But remember that God supplies all our needs, not "greeds."

The apostle Paul explained God's heavenly bank this way: "And my God [His promise is positive] shall supply [His promise is pointed] all your need [His promise is plentiful] according to His riches in glory by Christ Jesus" (Philippians 4:19). Notice that God doesn't supply "out of" His riches, but "according to" His riches in glory. We give our tithes and offerings "out of" available funds in the bank. God gives commensurate with His riches. His bank is colossal.

What are a couple of God's promises that are dearest to you at this point in your life? How can you live so that those you come in contact with daily will be drawn to the power and purpose of God's promises in you? Make this new year the beginning of a closer walk with God—by His divine power He has given you everything you need to live a godly life.

JANUARY 2
Treasure Caches

I rejoice at Your word as one who finds great treasure.
PSALM 119:162

Among new platforms and pursuits made possible by the digital revolution and smartphones, one of the most interesting is geocaching. Think of a treasure hunt—there are millions of "treasures" (caches) hidden by people all over the world. When you get directions via your smartphone and find the treasure, you make a record of your presence and leave the treasure for others to find and enjoy.

In the case of geocaching, the joy is more in the pursuit than in the treasure itself. Still, participants love the experience. The idea of a treasure map has always been the anticipated joy in discovering the treasure. In that way, the Bible is like a treasure map leading to the discovery of truth-based joy. In fact, the psalmist rejoiced at the anticipation of finding "great treasure" in God's Word. And what is the treasure? Salvation, security, the promises of God, instructions for living a joyful and godly life—who wouldn't rejoice at discovering such treasures?

The joy of discovery awaits all who read and obey the Word of God. Don't miss out on that joy by failing to know His Word.

My son, do not despise the chastening of the Lord, nor detest
His correction; for whom the Lord loves He corrects,
just as a father the son in whom he delights.

PROVERBS 3:11-12

In our humanity, we don't like to be corrected. Usually, the trials and chastening we experience are directed at us. But other times, we suffer the results of chastening directed by God toward others. That may not seem fair, but God is there to meet our needs even when we suffer from the result of others' actions.

That happened to the prophet Elijah. The northern tribes of Israel were deeply involved in idol worship and refused to repent. So God sent Elijah to King Ahab and warned him that rain would cease upon the land. That meant streams and springs would dry up, resulting in no agriculture or livestock. In short, a drought means no food for man or beast. As food dwindled in the land, God directed Elijah to set himself apart by a brook in the Cherith Ravine. There Elijah drank from the brook, which later dried up, and ravens brought him bread and meat every morning and evening. The drought wasn't Elijah's fault, and God provided for him until it was over.

Chastening is a school. Whatever its cause, God will use it to build our faith in Him.

JANUARY 4
Be Strong

My soul melts from heaviness; strengthen me according to Your word.
PSALM 119:28

For defendants in a courtroom, the rule of law makes all the difference. They are judged according to the law—not according to opinion or vengeance. The law contains provisions and protections, and defendants are tried and sentenced, or set free, according to the law—that is, based on the provisions written into the law.

That is a helpful way to think about the psalmist's words in Psalm 119:28: "Strengthen me according to Your word." The Word of God contains provisions and protections for the one who lives by it. The Bible tells us what is true about God—the provisions He has made for our well-being and the protection He offers those who dwell in Christ. Therefore, when we face times of weakness in life, we can be strengthened by reminding ourselves of the promises, provisions, and protections found in His Word (2 Peter 1:4). Like the psalmist, we can be strengthened according to God's Word.

If you are feeling weak or discouraged today, open God's Word to the verses cited in this devotional. Meditate on them and embrace the strength God provides.

JANUARY 5
He Is Preparing a Place for Us

In My Father's house are many mansions .... I go to prepare a place for you.
JOHN 14:2

There are countless tragedies occurring in our world—famines, civil wars, and natural disasters just to name a few. Our nation is attacking Christians more than ever before and our morals seem to be deteriorating. More people are leaving the Church and turning to the ideologies of our secular culture. How do we find hope in these times?

The world has always been plagued by sin. The Bible is filled with examples of heroes that lived in immoral cultures—Noah, Lot, Elijah, Joseph, Daniel, Shadrach, Meshach, Abed-Nego, and many more. Though it is easy to lose hope when we look at what is happening around us, we must remember we are not of this world—this is not our eternal home (Philippians 3:20).

The Lord is preparing a place for each of His children—a place so perfect our earthly minds cannot grasp the magnificence of it. And one day, when our time has come, our Father will say to us, "Well done, good and faithful servant" (Matthew 25:23) and welcome us into our eternal home.

So, let us set our hope in Jesus Christ and His glory and keep living for that day!

JANUARY 6
No Greater Joy

I have no greater joy than to hear that my children walk in truth.
3 JOHN 1:4

Parents delight in seeing their children make wise choices. Teachers delight in students grasping new concepts. Coaches delight in players successfully running a play. Orchestra conductors delight in musicians playing in harmony with one another. And the apostle John's delight, his joy, came from knowing other Christians were faithfully following the Lord.

Our faithfulness and perseverance in the Christian life brings glory to God and joy to those who have invested in our life spiritually. What joy floods our heart when a young person we discipled or taught enters full-time Christian ministry, marries a godly spouse, or becomes a leader in their local church! We may not see the spiritual growth take place in someone's life, but when we hear of the spiritual maturity of those we've invested in for years, we are filled with joy. This joy helps us stay the course and continue to invest in more lives. There is no greater joy in this life than seeing people's lives changed and watching them make an impact for eternity.

Most assuredly, I say to you, he who hears My word and believes
in Him who sent Me has everlasting life, and shall not come
into judgment, but has passed from death into life.

JOHN 5:24

Travel and Leisure Magazine ran an article on the "10 Most
Expensive Islands in the World." It takes a lot of time and
money, but if you have enough of both you may enjoy yourself
on Cocoa Island in the Maldives—the number one choice
because of its "mesmerizing beauty and pristine sand beaches."
But before booking your ticket, remember that the Maldives
is one of the most oppressive nations on earth for Christians.
According to Open Doors, radical Muslims control Maldivian
society, and any display of Christianity is forbidden.

God has promised a place of mesmerizing beauty for those
who hear His Word and believe in Him who sent Jesus Christ
to us. The glories of heaven far outstrip the exotic charm of the
world's richest islands. How tragic that those who live amid
great beauty don't recognize the Creator! While anticipating
the glories of heaven, we should be aware of the needs of earth.
While traveling through life, we should have a heart of mercy
for the nations.

JANUARY 8
Seize the Opportunity

*Then Philip opened his mouth, and beginning
at this Scripture, preached Jesus to him.*
ACTS 8:35

When Jimmy Carter was President of the United States, he visited Warsaw, Poland, which was under the domination of the Soviet Union. Carter engaged in discussions with First Secretary Edward Gierek, and afterward the Polish leader asked to speak to Carter privately. He was concerned about his spiritual condition. He told Carter that as a Communist, he embraced atheism, but that his mother was a Christian. It was clear the man was torn. Carter explained the Gospel to him and asked if he would consider accepting Jesus Christ as his personal Savior. Gierek explained that he was prohibited from making any public profession of faith.

Carter later said, "I never knew what his decision was about becoming a Christian before his death in 2001."[1]

We don't always see the results of our witness, but we never know when the opportunities will come. The Lord may open a door for you to share with someone today. Be ready to explain the Gospel and ask them if they would consider accepting Jesus Christ as their personal Savior. If the President of the United States can do it, so can you!

[1] Jimmy Carter, *A Full Life: Reflections at Ninety* (New York: Simon and Schuster, 2015), 133.

*Jesus replied, "You do not realize now what I am doing,
but later you will understand."*
JOHN 13:7, NIV

Betsie and Corrie ten Boom were sent to a concentration
camp for harboring Jews during World War II. They witnessed
horrible atrocities, but through it all they placed their hope in
the Lord. The sisters managed to sneak in a Bible and shared
God's Good News with other prisoners—they even led worship
services when they could. One of the many horrors the sisters
had to endure was that the barracks they were in were infested
with fleas. The bites were painful and frequent, but when
Corrie complained to Betsie, her sister would say, "Be thankful
for the fleas," knowing God had a purpose for everything.
Many years later, after leaving the camp, Corrie learned the
brutal guards didn't interrupt their worship services because
they refused to enter the flea-infested barracks.

   In the midst of turmoil, it is often difficult to understand
why the Lord allows certain things to happen to us. Though we
may never understand His purposes while on earth, we will
understand His purposes when we reach heaven. Betsie died
in the concentration camp, but some of her last words were,
"There is no pit so deep that He is not deeper still." Hold on to
that promise in the deepest valleys of your life, because God is
with you through it all.

JANUARY 10

The Lord Is a Warrior

You must not fear them, for the Lord your God Himself fights for you.
DEUTERONOMY 3:22

There will never be a problem you'll have to face alone. If you are a Christ-follower, you have a God who fights for you. Whatever is bothering you today, remember your Ally. The New Testament calls Him our Advocate (1 John 2:1) and says, "We are more than conquerors through Him who loved us" (Romans 8:37).

The Old Testament uses more militaristic words: *The Lord your God, who goes before you, He will fight for you, according to all He did for you in Egypt before your eyes* (Deuteronomy 1:30). *The Lord will fight for you, and you shall hold your peace* (Exodus 14:14). *You will not need to fight in this battle. Position yourselves, stand still and see the salvation of the Lord, who is with you* (2 Chronicles 20:17). *The battle is the Lord's* (1 Samuel 17:47). *The Lord is a man of war; the Lord is His name* (Exodus 15:3).

Calm down and remember the One who is by your side. He is a Warrior, an Advocate, and the One who lifts up our head (Psalm 3:3).

JANUARY 11
Roll Up Your Sleeves

And whatever you do, do it heartily, as to the Lord and not to men.
COLOSSIANS 3:23

Batwing, raglan, dolman, puffed, set-in, butterfly, paned, hanging, bell—these and more are styles of sleeves worn throughout history. Even today, the expression of someone "having something up his sleeve" refers to an Oriental-style hanging sleeve that was also used as a pocket—as still seen in China and Japan today. Today's long-sleeved shirts are often found to be overkill, as hard-working folks roll up their sleeves to accomplish their task.

Somehow, the idea of "working hard" as a Christian is lost on many believers, as if spiritual work should never be strenuous. Such a perspective might have drawn a stern correction from a hard worker like the apostle Paul. Not only did he set an example of giving one's all in service to Christ, he exhorted his readers to follow his example. We are to work heartily and be "steadfast, immovable, always abounding in the work of the Lord" (1 Corinthians 15:58). There is nothing about the Christian life that will not allow as much hard work as we want to give it.

Today, figuratively, if not literally, roll up your sleeves for the Kingdom's sake!

But [Jesus] answered and said, "It is written, 'Man shall not live by bread alone, but by every word that proceeds from the mouth of God.'"
MATTHEW 4:4

The judicial system, at least in courtroom trials, separates fact from fiction. That's not easy if two witnesses give contradictory accounts of the same event. But when there is hard evidence—a fingerprint, a surveillance tape, a DNA sample—the job of justice is made easier. A verifiable standard is what all other accounts must be measured by.

When Satan came to Jesus during His forty-day fast in the wilderness, he presented Jesus with three fictional scenarios. They were fictional because they were not part of Jesus' responsibility from His Father: to work miracles and test God for the sake of displaying divine power. So how did Jesus end the three tempting challenges? By quoting three verses from Deuteronomy that demonstrated the falsity of Satan's propositions. Satan's main weapon is lies—if not outright lies, then counterfeiting God's truth (Genesis 3:1-5; John 8:44). Truth puts flight to a lie every time.

God's Word is given so we might always know the truth about God, Satan, ourselves, and life. Use God's Word to put flight to temptations when they arise.

And the Angel of the Lord appeared to [Moses] in a flame of fire from the midst of a bush.

EXODUS 3:2

The phrase "the Angel of the Lord" with a capital "A" appears 52 times in the Old Testament but not once in the New Testament. Also, the phrase "an angel of the Lord" appears eleven times in the New Testament but not once in the Old Testament.

What do these pieces of information mean? The Angel of the Lord appears numerous times in the Old Testament, then Christ appears on earth, and the Angel of the Lord never appears again. This general observation leads Bible scholars to suggest that the Angel of the Lord was a theophany—a revelation of God Himself as the preincarnate Christ. Since God is Spirit (John 4:24), a visible manifestation of God in the Old Testament would be the second Person of the Trinity, Jesus Christ, in His preincarnate state. After being born physically, He ceases to appear as the Angel of the Lord.

The Angel of the Lord is just another example of God's continual care and presence as He made ready the revelation of Christ. We are constantly looked after, led and protected, by the God who loves us.

JANUARY 14
God's Peace

And let the peace of God rule in your hearts, to which also you were called in one body; and be thankful.

COLOSSIANS 3:15

Oswald Chambers wrote, "There are certain things we must not pray about—moods, for instance. Moods never go by praying, moods go by kicking." He wasn't telling us to never pray for better attitudes, but he was stating a basic emotional reality. We must take charge of our moods and kick the bad ones out of our hearts and minds. Just as importantly, we must open the door and usher in some better attitudes and let them rule in our hearts.

Gratitude is a choice we make. It's a command to obey, for the Bible tells us: "Be thankful." Remembering and reflecting on God's goodness is one of the blessings of thanksgiving. Take a moment and think about a situation that's causing you distress. Somewhere among the feelings of hurt, fear, anger, or anxiety—somewhere—there are some things for which to be thankful. What are they? List them, thank God for them, and let the peace of God rule in your heart.

God Makes a Way

You enlarged my path under me, so my feet did not slip.
PSALM 18:36

When Moses led the Hebrew slaves out of Egypt and headed for the Promised Land of Canaan, it could have been a short trip: follow the coastline of the Mediterranean Sea into Canaan. They would have immediately encountered the war-like Philistines who lived along the coast of Canaan and then fled straight back to Egypt. And there is no record of Moses telling the Hebrews this reasoning. They didn't understand what was happening, which ultimately led to much grumbling after they tired of the Sinai Desert (Exodus 13:17).

Sometimes God's directions and plans seem inconvenient, illogical, untimely—anything but what we might have desired or expected. For example, during the drought and resulting famine in Israel, God led Elijah to find food in the home of a poor widow who was prepared to use her last bit of flour and oil for bread, and then die. But God miraculously provided an unending supply for the woman, her son, and Elijah until the drought ended.

It was a strange way for God to provide, but it was provision! God enlarges our path, makes a way for us, even when the way seems unpredictable.

JANUARY 16
Small Space

The sun shall no longer be your light by day, nor for brightness shall the moon give light to you; but the Lord will be to you an everlasting light, and your God your glory.

ISAIAH 60:19

There's nothing worse than being stuck in a small, dark place. Whether we are trapped in a physical location or feeling intense internal pressure and chaos, discouragement sets in the moment we believe we are all alone and trapped indefinitely. We want a timeline for rescue and freedom. Thomas had given up hope. Even after he saw the other disciples' enthusiasm and confidence in the Resurrection of Christ, he had doubts. It was not until Christ appeared personally to him that his faith and courage were renewed.

God is not held back by physical barriers or internal darkness. He spoke the entire world into existence. Just as Christ appeared before Thomas, He longs to be with you, regardless of how dark your discouragement and circumstances are. Take a moment to invite Jesus to meet you. He cares for you. No place within you or surrounding you is too dark for God's light to shine.

But you are a chosen generation, a royal priesthood, a holy nation,
His own special people, that you may proclaim the praises of Him
who called you out of darkness into His marvelous light.

1 PETER 2:9

Anthony Bourdain, the globe-trotting television chef who took his own life, wrote in a memoir: "Your body is not a temple. It's an amusement park. Enjoy the ride." That's how Bourdain lived. He enjoyed, experienced, indulged, abused, ate, drank, and wandered around until his ride came to a tragic stop.

But our lives are *not* amusement rides; they are designed as temples for the Holy Spirit, who lives within us when Jesus Christ is our Lord and Savior. We are here on assignment, and Christ lives through us as we labor for glory.

Because of the resurrection of Christ, our time on earth is not futile. Our days are filled with hope and optimism because the One living within us overcame sin, death, the devil, and hell. We may never travel to the ends of the earth for television, but we represent a Savior who is reaching the ends of the earth with the Good News—and we are part of His program!

JANUARY 18
Watching Over Me

Are they not all ministering spirits sent forth to minister
for those who will inherit salvation?
HEBREWS 1:14

Pietro da Cortona (1596-1669) was an Italian painter and architect. One of his most famous paintings is *The Guardian Angel*, a lavish painting completed in 1656 of a beautiful female angel with wings holding the arm of a child as he walks on a path. The image of a guardian angel has occupied the imagination of countless artists through the years—the most frequent presentation is of an angel in a child's bedroom guarding the child as she sleeps.

Are such images biblical? Angels themselves certainly are, as is the idea of them guarding the children of God. Angels perform God's Word (Psalm 103:20) and are sent "to minister for those who will inherit salvation" (Hebrews 1:14). The song many children learn to sing—"All night, all day, angels watching over me"—lays the foundation for a serious biblical truth: Angels are God's ministering spirits whose assignment is to watch over His children.

Keep in mind—"all day and all night"—that you are being watched over by the angels of God. Give God thanks for His angelic protectors and live with conscious, spiritual awareness of their presence.

JANUARY 19
Every Moment, Every Day

Time is short.
1 CORINTHIANS 7:29

Two Washington, D.C., residents quit their jobs to bicycle around the world. Jay Austin and Lauren Geoghegan described their adventures on their blog, "Simply Cycling," explaining, "Because life is short and the world is big ... we want to make the most out of our youth and good health before they're gone." Tragically they were killed by ISIS terrorists while bicycling in Tajikistan. They were 29.

We know time is short, but we don't always know how short it is. The writer of Psalm 89:47 says, "Remember how short my time is." For those who know Jesus as Savior, our life in Christ extends throughout all eternity—we have heaven and all of eternity to spend with our Savior and Lord. But we have a brief allocation of time on earth, and we don't have a certain promise of even another day.

Let's make the most of the moments God gives us. Don't fritter your time away with endless diversions and distractions. Live purposefully, making the most of the opportunities because the days are evil (Ephesians 5:16). Let's take advantage of every moment and every day for Christ and His kingdom.

JANUARY 20
Choose the Best

But seek first the kingdom of God and His righteousness,
and all these things shall be added to you.
MATTHEW 6:33

Do you remember your grammar lessons? In English, two types of adjectives are comparative and superlative. Comparative adjectives rank two different nouns: "Jim is the taller of the two boys." Superlative adjectives compare a noun to a group at either the upper end or lower end, "Jim is the tallest of all" or "Tom is the smallest of all." Akin to these rankings are a set of three adjectives that are more subjective: good, better, and best.

In life we would like everything to be clear-cut, making choices easy: good or bad, black or white, yes or no. In reality, most of life—including the Christian life—is more subjective. Among all the options, how do we know if what we do with our time, talent, and treasure is good, better, or best? How do we set priorities for our life? Today is a good day to seek wisdom to make the best choices possible through prayer, Scripture, and wise counsel.

Jesus said the best choice is always to make God's Kingdom our priority, our best choice. Everything else will fall into place accordingly.

JANUARY 21
One Resolution

For now we see in a mirror, dimly, but then face to face. Now I know in part, but then I shall know just as I also am known.
1 CORINTHIANS 13:12

Most people make New Year's resolutions, but research shows that most people don't achieve them. The month has already begun, but perhaps today would be a good day to think about simplifying the idea of making a resolution for this year. How? By making only one.

There is one resolution guaranteed to be achievable and impact all your other goals for 2020: Seek wisdom from God every day. By achieving that goal, many other unmade resolutions will find fulfillment. One of the Old Testament meanings of wisdom referred to skill; a wise person was skilled in living (see the book of Proverbs). If we ask God for wisdom, He will provide it (James 1:5). And if God provides wisdom, then every day we will become more skilled at living life in a way that is fruitful and honoring to God. When we ask for wisdom and are serious about applying it, then all of life becomes better: finances, personal goals, relationships, direction for the future, marriage and family—everything.

We see life dimly now, like looking through a dark glass. Therefore, we need wisdom to see more clearly. Ask God for wisdom today and every day of this year.

JANUARY 22
Pray Shamelessly

I say to you, though he will not rise and give to him because he is his friend,
yet because of his persistence he will rise and give him as many as he needs.
LUKE 11:8

A young, first-time mother feels overwhelmed with the task of carrying for her newborn. Both her own mother and mother-in-law live nearby, and she has called them repeatedly for advice and help. One day, when her baby is wailing in discomfort, she wants to call them again. But she thinks, "I'm too embarrassed—no, ashamed—to call and ask for help again!"

Who hasn't felt that way—even when we go to God in prayer? Jesus described a man who felt no shame in asking for help. This man knocked on his neighbor's door in the middle of the night to ask for bread to feed a later-arriving traveler. The neighbor, not happy at being disturbed, finally got up and gave him the bread because of the man's "lack of shame" in asking (translated "persistence" or "boldness" in English translations). But the Greek word means "having no shame." Jesus told the story to illustrate how we should pray—shamelessly, boldly, courageously.

Do you ever lack confidence in your prayers? Remember, God invites us to pray boldly (Hebrews 4:16). There is no shame in asking repeatedly when we are invited to do so.

JANUARY 23
Amazing Faith

When Jesus heard these things, He marveled at [the Roman centurion], and turned around and said to the crowd that followed Him, "I say to you, I have not found such great faith, not even in Israel!"

LUKE 7:9

A first-year junior associate is called to the office of the law firm's senior partner—an intimidating experience. From behind the partner's walnut desk come these words: "I have to say, Robert, I am amazed at the quality of your work." What did he mean? Was that a good "amazed" or a bad "amazed"?

It depends on the context. Jesus illustrated His own amazement—both kinds—regarding faith. On the one hand, a Roman soldier demonstrated faith that Jesus could heal the soldier's sick servant by just saying the word. Jesus was amazed (He "marveled") at that kind of faith. On the other hand, when Jesus went to His own hometown, many who knew Him were offended by His teachings—"they were offended at Him" (Mark 6:3). "And He marveled [was amazed] because of their unbelief" (Mark 6:6). So in one case, Jesus was amazed at the presence of faith; in another case, He was amazed at the lack of it.

You will amaze Jesus one way or the other by your faith—either its presence or its absence. Make sure He is amazed by the unshakeable nature of your faith.

JANUARY 24
Finding Your Purpose

But when it pleased God, who separated me from my
mother's womb and called me through His grace.
GALATIANS 1:15

A chiropractic doctor was participating in a triathlon when he was struck by a vehicle. With severe injuries to his back, his doctors suggested he might not walk again. But twelve weeks later he was back in training. What he discovered about the potential of the human heart, soul, mind, and body to recover from trauma became his new life purpose—sharing a message of recovery and potential to worldwide audiences.

Sometimes life purposes are revealed in surprising ways. Take the apostle Paul, who thought his life purpose was to be a scholarly rabbi in first-century Judaism. Then, an encounter with the resurrected Christ cast a new light on his brilliance and scholarship. He suddenly realized God had set him apart from birth to take the Gospel of Christ to the Gentile world— something he would have been far less equipped to do without his prior scholarly training.

Life purpose has two parts: today and tomorrow. Trust God for grace to fulfill the purpose He has for you today (spouse, parent, employee, employer) while being attentive to how your purpose might grow and develop as your life unfolds. Pray that God will reveal His purpose for you through good times and bad (Romans 8:28-29).

JANUARY 25
Small Actions

Yet I considered it necessary to send to you Epaphroditus,
my brother, fellow worker, and fellow soldier, but your
messenger and the one who ministered to my need.

PHILIPPIANS 2:25

One of the most popular documentaries in the British Broadcasting Corporation's history is the ten-episode series called *Connections* (1978). The series was created by, and featured, science historian James Burke who explained the coincidental twists and turns in the history of science and technology. A seemingly random event often resulted in a major breakthrough years later.

We often overlook seemingly small or inconsequential events—and people—in God's history, a history in which there is nothing random or meaningless. Take Epaphroditus, for example, a member of the church in Philippi. He is mentioned only twice in Scripture (Philippians 2:25; 4:18), but his "small" act of courage may have radically preserved the life of the apostle Paul. While Paul was in prison, Epaphroditus travelled from Philippi to Rome with supplies for the apostle. Was it food? Medicine? Warm clothing? Other supplies? Whatever it was, Paul lavished praise on this man whose sacrificial efforts might have preserved Paul's life (Philippians 2:17).

Never underestimate the power of small actions in life. God uses them all for His purposes and glory. What seems like an insignificant word or action on our part may set in motion a chain of events that God uses in a mighty way.

JANUARY 26
Rescue Mission

[God] has delivered us from the power of darkness and
conveyed us into the kingdom of the Son of His love.
COLOSSIANS 1:13

For seventeen days in 2018, the world watched as the fate of
a Thai youth soccer team hung in the balance—trapped deep
underground in a dark cave. For nearly three weeks, specialists
planned how to extricate the twelve boys and their coach from
their dark prison. None of the news accounts used mild words
like "transfer" or "deliver" to describe the mission. Instead,
they used the only word that applied: *Rescue!*

Rescue is what Paul had in mind when he wrote that God
delivered (rescued) us from the domain of darkness to the
kingdom of Christ. This was no mere transaction, moving souls
from the "lost" ledger to the "saved" ledger. It was a rescue!
One wonders if Paul had in mind God's rescue of the Hebrew
slaves from Egypt—a domain of darkness if ever there was one
(Exodus 6:6; 14:30). It's why some modern English versions
use "rescued" instead of "delivered" in their translation of
Colossians 1:13.

No one would ever forget being rescued from a cave or a
burning building. But do we remember the dramatic rescue
God performed when He brought us out of darkness into
eternal light and life? Thank God today for rescuing your soul
by His love.

This Book of the Law shall not depart from your mouth, but you shall meditate in it day and night, that you may observe to do according to all that is written in it. For then you will make your way prosperous, and then you will have good success.

JOSHUA 1:8

In 1955, a Harvard medical doctor published a paper titled "The Powerful Placebo." Dr. Henry Beecher said that placebos—inert substances designed to encourage a patient's sense that good things were going to happen—are clinically significant. Promises, and our confidence in the promise-maker, play a significant role in our success.

When Joshua was tasked by God with the mission of settling Israel in the Promised Land, he had two resources: God and His promises. Those promises were contained in the Book of the Law that Moses had compiled. In that Book were God's covenant promises to Israel: Walk in God's precepts, and God will be your provider and defender. Reminding himself of those promises, along with the record of God's faithfulness in the exodus from Egypt, was Joshua's means to success. Meditating on God's Word daily kept God and His promises front and center.

Like Joshua, we have been given "exceedingly great and precious promises" that will ensure our spiritual success in life (2 Peter 1:4). And like Joshua, our success depends on taking God at His Word "day and night."

JANUARY 28
Eyes on God

O our God, will You not judge them? For we have no power
against this great multitude that is coming against us; nor
do we know what to do, but our eyes are upon You.
2 CHRONICLES 20:12

The downfall of American President Richard M. Nixon
remains a dark period in the nation's history. Author Tim
Weiner captured how Nixon must have felt with the title of
his bestselling book: *One Man Against the World: The Tragedy of*
Richard Nixon (2015). There are times in everyone's life when it
seems the world is against them.

King Jehoshaphat of Judah surely felt that way when three
neighboring nations came against Judah. Jehoshaphat prayed,
imploring the Lord to defeat their enemies (2 Chronicles 20:5-
12). In short, Jehoshaphat was saying, "We are alone in the
world. The whole world is arrayed against us. Only You can save
us." The final words of the king's prayer sum up how every child
of God should respond: "Nor do we know what to do, *but our*
eyes are upon You" (emphasis added). God answered the king's
prayer and delivered Judah in a mighty victory, after which
there was much rejoicing in the land.

If it is "you against the world" today, keep your eyes on
God and His promises. When you don't know what to do,
God does! And He will lead you as you fix your eyes on Jesus
(Hebrews 12:2).

And the peace of God, which surpasses all understanding, will guard your hearts and minds through Christ Jesus.

PHILIPPIANS 4:7

According to the Anxiety and Depression Association of America, forty million adults (age eighteen and over) in America suffer from anxiety disorders—more than eighteen percent of the adult population. These disorders are serious, evoking compassion for those who suffer. If we could give a non-medical gift to all who are anxious, it would have to be the gift of peace.

When Jesus was about to leave the earth, He knew His disciples would be "anxious" about His departure, so young were they in their understanding. To combat their anxiety, He gave them a gift: "Peace I leave with you, My peace I give to you …. Let not your heart be troubled" (John 14:27). Though the apostle Paul was not among those to whom Jesus spoke, he surely must have heard about Jesus' parting words. He wrote something similar to the Philippians: "Be anxious for nothing, but in everything by prayer and supplication, with thanksgiving, let your requests be made known to God; and the peace of God … will guard your hearts and minds through Christ Jesus" (Philippians 4:6-7).

Peace comes through prayer and the replacement of anxious thoughts with peaceful thoughts (Philippians 4:8) by which "the God of peace will be with you" (Philippians 4:9).

He must increase, but I must decrease.
JOHN 3:30

In 1969, management principles set forth by Dr. Laurence J. Peter were published in the book, *The Peter Principle*. The book suggested that employees are often promoted beyond their level of competence. That is, better to know what you're good at than to be promoted into responsibilities which reveal your incompetence.

John the Baptist was a man who knew exactly what his role was. He was very good at what God had called him to do and never demonstrated a desire to be "promoted" higher. John's mission was to be the herald, the forerunner, of the coming Jewish Messiah, Jesus of Nazareth. Despite being a cousin of Jesus, John never demonstrated any sense of rivalry or jealousy toward Jesus; John never wondered why he was not the Messiah. John's own disciples were more ambitious than their teacher; they resented Jesus' growing popularity. But John reminded them that his great joy was to receive heaven's assignment, suggesting they should do the same. In fact, John knew his own notoriety would decrease as Jesus' mission increased. He said as much: "[Jesus] must increase, but I must decrease."

There is great wisdom in knowing our place in God's Kingdom. If God opens doors and marks out a path, by all means we should proceed. But we should never force doors open out of our own ambition. Pray—then proceed.

JANUARY 31
The Best Seat

*For whoever exalts himself will be humbled, and
he who humbles himself will be exalted.*

LUKE 14:11

"Networking" has become a refined skill. People attend civic
meetings, volunteer for community service, even attend church
looking for opportunities to meet those who can help them
succeed in business. Is that wrong?

Jesus attended a Sabbath meal in the home of a prominent
Pharisee. Watching the guests as they arrived for the meal,
Jesus noticed "how they chose the best [seats]" for themselves
(Luke 14:7)—seats that would be advantageous to them in
terms of prestige. So He told the crowd a parable about a
wedding feast and explained how inadvisable it was to seek the
best seat. Why? Because if a very important guest arrived after
you, the host might have to ask you to move and take a lesser
seat. How embarrassing! Better, Jesus said, to take the lesser
seat to begin with and wait for the host (God, in this case) to
exalt you to a higher place in His time (Luke 14:8-11). There
might have been a bit of this "maneuvering for advantage" at
Jesus' Last Supper with His own disciples—they were arguing
among themselves as to who was most important (Luke 22:24).

Jesus' summary: Better to humble ourselves than to have
God humble us. If it's time to have a better seat at the table,
God will make it happen.

FEBRUARY

FEBRUARY 1
Looking to the Future

So I will restore to you the years that the swarming locust has eaten,
the crawling locust, the consuming locust, and the chewing locust,
My great army which I sent among you.

JOEL 2:25

Most adults will admit: "My parents' discipline was worth it.
I didn't see it then, but I see it now." That is, discipline done
correctly always leads to better outcomes. God's discipline is
always motivated by His love (Hebrews 12:3-11).

All of Israel was experiencing an unprecedented drought
and infestation of locusts (Joel 1:2-4). The winged insects
arrived as clouds of eating machines, blown by the wind
across the face of an entire nation. They stripped the crops
and trees bare, ruining the harvest for an entire season (1:10-
12). The prophet Joel knew it was because of Israel's sins that
God was using locusts and drought to discipline them. In
fact, Moses had warned Israel that God would do just a thing
(Deuteronomy 28:42). But in Joel's words and God's acts of
judgment and discipline, there was a redemptive thread: "I will
restore to you the years that the swarming locust has eaten." If
Israel would turn back to God, His blessings would return as
well.

If you find yourself being trained (disciplined) by God,
know that it is only for a season if you will receive it in faith.
God always looks to the future.

FEBRUARY 2
Whatever You Do

*And whatever you do in word or deed, do all in the name of the
Lord Jesus, giving thanks to God the Father through Him.*
COLOSSIANS 3:17

The apostle Paul was a brilliant man. His training would have
likely qualified him for a modern law degree and doctorates
in biblical studies and pastoral ministry. He was a scholar and
intellectual with a pastor's heart.

But what are we to make of his eventual reflection that
his training—the best Judaism had to offer in his day (Acts
22:3; Galatians 1:14)—was all loss compared to knowing Christ
(Philippians 3:4-9)? Doing it over, would Paul never have
trained as an up and coming rabbi in Judaism—a Pharisee
of Pharisees? What about us—should we pursue advanced
academic training, or is it too "worldly"? Answer: Think how
the New Testament might have been different if Paul had not
been trained in the Law and the Old Testament. God used Paul's
intellect and training to write the documents that shaped, and
continue to shape, the Church! Once Paul met Christ, he saw
the relevance of using God's gifts for the glory of Christ, not
the glory of man. And we should do the same.

Stewardship means being faithful to use the gifts of God,
whatever they are (1 Corinthians 4:2). "Whatever you do, do all
to the glory of God" (1 Corinthians 10:31).

How to Hope

Now hope does not disappoint, because the love of God has been poured out in our hearts by the Holy Spirit who was given to us.

ROMANS 5:5

If you watch the evening news, read the daily newspaper, or scroll the Internet for the latest news, no doubt you will become discouraged. Strife, hatred, and division seem to be the events that are reported upon most often. But praise God, our hope is not to be found in the daily news reports; it is in God.

When do we most need hope? In times of suffering. It is in those times that we are most tempted to give up and to lose heart. The apostle Paul knew this and wrote about hope in the context of suffering. He explained how suffering can lead to hope: "And not only that, but we also glory in tribulations, knowing that tribulation produces perseverance; and perseverance, character; and character, hope" (Romans 5:3-4). From suffering to hope via perseverance and character. *And hope does not disappoint!* Christian hope is rooted solidly in the love of God poured into our hearts by the Holy Spirit for all who are in Christ.

Nobody likes to suffer; everybody needs hope. Hope is what carries us through suffering to the future God has in store. If you are hurting today, let your pain lead you to hope in God.

The righteous. … shall still bear fruit in old age;
they shall be fresh and flourishing.

PSALM 92:12-14

The idea of retirement from an active working life is a modern development—late nineteenth and early twentieth centuries. Pensions and government retirement provisions began making it possible for people to have income without working. In most countries today, the expected retirement age is between 60–65, though it is gradually increasing due to increasing lifespans.

The problem with the modern notion of retiring from active *work* is that, too often, retirement from active *life* goes with it. The senior season of life is seen by many to be a contracting period in contrast to the expanding period from ages 20–65. But should it be? There is no biblical precedent for such thinking. Scripture suggests fruitfulness throughout life, death being a gathering to God at the peak of the harvest (Job 5:26). When Mary and Joseph took the baby Jesus to the temple as an infant, they encountered two godly senior saints—Simeon and Anna—who were anything but retired (Luke 2:25-38). They spent time worshiping in the temple in Jerusalem, praying and waiting for the Messiah to appear. Their senior years were devoted to serving God.

Whatever your age today, don't be fooled into thinking life ends at 65. Prepare now, mentally and spiritually, to continue bearing fruit throughout your senior season.

FEBRUARY 5
Pleasing Him

Walk worthy of the Lord, fully pleasing Him, being fruitful in
every good work and increasing in the knowledge of God.
COLOSSIANS 1:10

Newly married couples are just beginning the journey of
learning how to bring joy and happiness to their spouse's life.
The longer they are married, the more they know about their
spouse. As the years pass, a husband learns how much his wife
appreciates when he cleans the kitchen for her, and a wife
learns how much her husband is encouraged when she sits
down with him and watches his favorite sports team play.

As Christians we are called to be "fully pleasing to [the
Lord]" (Colossians 1:10), to be acceptable to Him in all we say
and do. In order to live this way, we need to get to know God
and His Word. Knowledge of God's Word means we know what
pleases Him, just like knowledge of our spouse means we know
how to love them better. As our knowledge of God increases
and becomes part of who we are, we please Him more and
more through our fruitful character and conduct.

The entirety of Your Word is truth.
PSALM 119:160

When you change news channels, you change worldviews. Journalism is now so opinionated that the same story, reported by two different broadcasters, sounds like totally different events. We switch stations and ask, "Are these people on the same planet? What happened to objective news? How do we know what to believe?"

As you form your opinions, make sure to build your worldview on the basis of Scripture. In John's Gospel, Jesus said, "I am the way, the truth, and the life" (14:6). He called the Holy Spirit the "Spirit of truth" (14:17). He prayed to the Father, "Sanctify them by Your truth. Your word is truth" (17:17).

Christians who study their Bibles every day, who memorize God's Word, who meditate on His precepts, and who accept the authority of Scripture are less likely to be deceived. They are like treasury agents who can detect a counterfeit bill because they are well-versed in the genuine article. When surrounded by half-truths and lies, we can feel confused, but the solution isn't giving up. We must give the situation to God and seek His truth.

FEBRUARY 7
Landmines

The pride of your heart has deceived you.
OBADIAH 1:3

"Each morning, the enemy lays out his landmines in our lives," wrote Dr. Charles Stanley. "If we are not discerning, we will fall prey to his tactics. The landmine of pride can tear a gaping hole in the life of the person who yields to its folly. It is one of Satan's chief modes of operation and favorite weapons of warfare because it tempts us to take our eyes off God and place them on ourselves."[2]

Pride is so deceptive that it destroyed the reputation of the powerful angel, Lucifer, who said, "I will ascend into heaven, I will exalt my throne above the stars of God" (Isaiah 14:13). The sin of pride and arrogance caused Satan to become the epitome of evil today. It's a reminder that we should never seek to be above others, but to serve as Christ served.

If you have gifts, accomplishments, honors, blessings, and influence, make them matters of thanksgiving and recognize them as gifts from God to use in the service of Christ. Keep your eyes on Jesus and live a life of humble thanksgiving and Christ-centered service.

---

[2] Charles F. Stanley, *Landmines in the Path of the Believer* (Nashville: Thomas Nelson, 2007), 14.

John the Eccentric

Now John was clothed with camel's hair and with a leather belt around his waist, and he ate locusts and wild honey.

MARK 1:6

The patience of parents is often tested during their children's teenage years. But what if that teenage child never grows out of his or her eccentric ways and becomes a young adult who just doesn't seem to fit in? That was the challenge faced by the parents of John the Baptist.

The angel Gabriel appeared to John's father, Zacharias, and told him of the special role his son would have. He would bring "joy and gladness" in the role to which God would call him, but his role would be different: He would be like Elijah the prophet as a forerunner to the coming Messiah (Luke 1:13-17). Prophets were a breed apart in Israel, often living lives of exclusion and even danger. When John entered into the fullness of his ministry, he lived in the wilderness and wore a prophet's garb and ate strange foods. At some point, John's parents were forced to let go of their child and let him fulfill God's call.

God's creation is filled with uniqueness and variety. Surely that applies to those called to serve Him as well.

I say to you that likewise there will be more joy in heaven over one sinner who repents than over ninety-nine just persons who need no repentance.

LUKE 15:7

A daredevil raccoon, searching for bird eggs, kept animal lovers on edge when it scaled a 25-story skyscraper in St. Paul, Minnesota, and became stuck near the top. Television cameras followed the drama closely. Workers finally rescued the creature when it reached the roof and released it safely. One raccoon behavior expert said, "Raccoons don't think ahead very much, so raccoons don't have very good impulse control. I don't think the raccoon realized when it started climbing what it was in for."

That sounds like a lot of humans, doesn't it?

We are so prone to head in the wrong direction, make mistakes, fail to think ahead, and often fail to exercise impulse control. We get ourselves trapped by life.

But we have Someone who can rescue us. Through Jesus Christ, who died on the cross to give us victory over our sin, we've received the gift of righteousness and are no longer chained to the cycle of sin and guilt. Every time Jesus rescues a soul, it should be a sensation. It's truly a celebration in heaven.

The lazy man says, "There is a lion outside! I shall be slain in the streets!"
PROVERBS 22:13

A neighborhood in New York City went into a frenzy over reports of a tiger in the streets. The police got the call about 8:30 a.m., and the news swept through the area. People brought in their children and locked their doors as authorities mounted an intensive search. But it turns out there was no tiger. It was a raccoon.

When our faith gets lazy and we aren't trusting God as we should, every raccoon looks like a tiger. But when we're walking with God and are confident in His promises, everything returns to its proper perspective. Proverbs 28:1 says, "The wicked flee when no one pursues, but the righteous are bold as a lion."

If you're worried about something happening around you, turn to God in faith and respond to Him in righteousness. No one can lay hands on God's anointed unless he is given permission to do so. God is ever present with us.

*Do not forget to entertain strangers, for by so doing
some have unwittingly entertained angels.*

HEBREWS 13:2

One verse in the Bible has the potential to transform our daily
life. Hebrews 13:2 says that some of the people we encounter
in our daily life may look like humans but are, in fact, angels.
Angels! That's all it says—no instructions on how to tell when
an angel appears and when a person is, in fact, just a person.
But there it is: an admonition to hospitality to strangers since
that stranger might just be an angel in disguise.

Angels appeared to various people in the Old Testament:
Abraham (Genesis 18), Gideon (Judges 6), and Manoah (Judges
13). The angel Gabriel appeared to Daniel, but the text uses the
word "man" to describe him (Daniel 8:15; 9:21). And in Daniel
10, "a certain man" appeared to Daniel with a message from
heaven (verses 5-9). Because the primary function of an angel is
to be a messenger, their appearance is likely to be suited to the
occasion or the recipient of the message.

The fact that angels are among us compels us to be
hospitable (kind, loving) to everyone regardless of who we
think they are.

We do not look at the things which are seen,
but at the things which are not seen.
2 CORINTHIANS 4:18

We need filters to strain certain questions from invading our thoughts. For example, the question *Why?* is natural and normal, but sometimes only God knows the answer. When we obsess with the *Whys*, we might forget the *Who*. And what about the phrases, *If only ...* and *What if ...?* Those, too, are normal; but again, only God can answer them. He does not want your thoughts to torment you. He stands ready to forgive your sins and to bring good from your mistakes. The sufferings of this present world are not worth comparing to the glories to be revealed.

The Bible says, "You will keep him in perfect peace, whose mind is stayed on You, because he trusts in You. Trust in the Lord forever, for in Yah, the Lord, is everlasting strength" (Isaiah 26:3-4).

Too often our thoughts are seized by the unanswerable questions of life, but how vital to turn our minds to the unsearchable God who knows the answers, will reveal them in due time, and can work all things for the good of His children.

Trust Him today.

A New Leaf

Let every man be swift to hear, slow to speak, slow to wrath; for the wrath of
man does not produce the righteousness of God.
JAMES 1:19-20

When you think of turning over a new leaf, perhaps you envision a leaf from a tree, but that's not what the expression means. Back in the 1500s, pages of books were called leaves. Turning over a new leaf meant turning to a blank page to begin again. Every day we have the opportunity to turn the page and start afresh.

For example, perhaps you'd like to be less irritable. Many people are irritable because they're tired, so a new bedtime routine might help. Some are angry because they've allowed bitterness to accrue in their hearts, so they might want to ask God for a forgiving spirit.

Sometimes we're irritable just because we've learned patterns of impatience. In that case, set a goal of memorizing James 1:19-20: "My dear brothers and sisters, take note of this: Everyone should be quick to listen, slow to speak and slow to become angry, because human anger does not produce the righteousness that God desires" (NIV).

The best way of turning over some new leaves is by leaving anger behind—and the leaves of Scripture can help you with that.

FEBRUARY 14
Good Things

He who finds a wife finds a good thing, and obtains favor from the Lord.
PROVERBS 18:22

God specializes in good things. Moses told the Israelites, "So you shall rejoice in every good thing which the Lord your God has given to you and your house" (Deuteronomy 26:11). Joshua said, "Not a word failed of any good thing which the Lord had spoken" (Joshua 21:45). Psalm 34:10 says, "Those who seek the Lord shall not lack any good thing." Psalm 84:11 adds, "No good thing will He withhold from those who walk uprightly." Paul told Timothy, "That good thing which was committed to you, keep by the Holy Spirit" (2 Timothy 1:14).

According to Proverbs 18:22, having a husband or wife is a "good thing," but we must guard the relationship committed to us. The foundation of a good marriage begins with knowing and loving God. As we grow in Christ, He gives us the spiritual resources we need to bring patience, joy, and faithfulness into our home. Marriage is really a three-way friendship between a man, a woman, and the Lord. We must be zealous to guard that.

Galatians 4:18 says, "It is good to be zealous in a good thing always."

FEBRUARY 15
Wise Counsel

*Without counsel, plans go awry, but in the multitude
of counselors they are established.*
PROVERBS 15:22

Roughly speaking, around 2.5 million people work for the
American federal government in some capacity. Theoretically,
all of those individuals have the ear of the President of the
United States through the President's Cabinet—the heads
of fifteen executive departments (State, Defense, Treasury,
and more), plus the Vice President. Eight other counselors
attend Cabinet meetings but are not official Cabinet members.
Then, the President has a roster of hand-picked White House
advisors. Finally, every citizen can give the President advice
through their Congresspersons and Senators.

The Founding Fathers' idea was that the Executive leader
of the United States was to be held in check by an abundance
of counselors. And that idea—a "multitude of counselors"—is
thoroughly biblical. Even King Solomon, a royal monarch,
knew there was value in the accountability and wisdom
of many counselors. The same surely holds true for us as
individuals.

Who are your wise counselors? What kind of access do you
allow them in your life? Purpose to live a life filled with wise
counsel. Seek out godly friends and mentors who can help you
make the wisest decisions and whose counsel you are prepared
to take.

FEBRUARY 16
All the Time

Rejoice always, pray without ceasing, in everything give thanks;
for this is the will of God in Christ Jesus for you.
1 THESSALONIANS 5:16-18

When preaching on the Ten Commandments, preachers like to remind their listeners that "God didn't give us ten suggestions; He gave us Ten Commandments." It's easy to read the English text of the Bible without realizing the imperative, or command, mode of some verses.

Take 1 Thessalonians 5:16-18 where three exhortations are given: "Rejoice ... pray ... give thanks." We could read these as suggestions, even exhortations, and miss the fact that in the Greek language they are imperative commands. Paul even drives that point home by saying, "this is the will of God in Christ Jesus for you." Rejoicing always, praying continually, and giving thanks in everything are God's will for His people. "Why?" we might ask. Because we trust that God is watching over our lives continually; that whatever happens comes through the filter of His will—His goodness and love. Even if things are difficult, we can trust Him.

Make 2020 a year of rejoicing, praying, and giving thanks—all the time, in everything! This is the will of God in Christ Jesus for you.

FEBRUARY 17
God's Tapestry

And we know that all things work together for good to those who love God,
to those who are the called according to His purpose.
ROMANS 8:28

Today, parents are hesitant to say one of their children is a favorite. But in the ancient world, this was not the case. Jacob (Israel), for example, loved Joseph more than his eleven other sons since Joseph had been born in Jacob's old age to Rachel, Jacob's favorite wife (Genesis 37:3). As a sign of his favoritism, Jacob gave Joseph a beautiful robe "of many colors." All this favoritism provoked jealousy among Joseph's brothers and they sold him into slavery in Egypt. When the brothers were united many years later, Joseph blessed God for how He had worked in all their lives.

Our lives are multicolored, a tapestry held together on the backside by knots and stitches. Yet out of that which appears random and tenuous on one side, God creates a life of beauty on the other side through redemption in Christ.

No one's life is perfect, but God causes all the hard parts to be woven together for His glory. Give God thanks today for the "life of many colors" He is making for you as His beloved child.

FEBRUARY 18
Heavenly Sunlight

Seek the Lord and His strength; seek His face evermore!
PSALM 105:4

A limited amount of time spent in the sun has its benefits—increased levels of vitamin D and serotonin are two of them. But to keep the benefits, the exposure needs to be continued. When the disciples spent time with Jesus, they were changed, too. As they witnessed the life of Jesus, His preaching, and the miracles He performed, it would be easy to assume that faith came easily to them. It did not. Despite being physically close to Jesus and His power, the disciples struggled to believe and accept His identity as the Son of God and the unstoppable nature of His love and power. Waves and challenges quickly discouraged the disciples and pulled their gaze away from Christ.

The narrative running throughout the Gospels reveals the importance of keeping our eyes and attention on God, regardless of the situations being faced. Instead of looking at our physical surroundings and circumstances, we need to focus our attention on the Lord and His strength. Nothing can thwart His promises or purpose. As we bask in the truth of His Word and the power of His presence, we are set free.

Faith in Faithless Times

But the righteous shall live by his faith.
HABAKKUK 2:4, ESV

The prophet Habakkuk left us an interesting book. Its three short chapters are essentially a counseling session between Habakkuk and God, for the prophet was troubled by the turbulent times in which he lived. He couldn't understand why his culture had crumbled and why the streets of his city had become so lawless, so godless. He prayed about it in chapter 1; and in chapter 2, God told Habakkuk to trust Him and to live by faith (verse 4), for "the Lord is in His holy temple," and one day "the earth will be filled with the knowledge of the glory of the Lord, as the waters cover the sea" (verses 20, 14).

In response Habakkuk composed a hymn of rejoicing in his third and final chapter, saying, "The Lord God is my strength; He will make my feet like deer's feet, and He will make me walk on my high hills" (verse 19).

When the way becomes rough, trust Him who is still in His holy temple. He will give you hinds' feet on high places.

For out of the heart proceed evil thoughts, murders, adulteries,
fornications, thefts, false witness, blasphemies.
MATTHEW 15:19

Mao Zedong believed sparrows were pests, so he initiated a campaign to eradicate sparrows in China. But he was wrong. Sparrows are natural predators to locusts. With the sparrows all gone, the locusts multiplied, devastating Chinese agriculture. It's estimated that more than thirty million Chinese died of malnourishment because of Mao Zedong's defective thinking.

Defective thinking results in destructive living. It's impossible to think wrongly and live rightly, which is the problem with the human race. Our evil hearts produce evil thoughts, and all kinds of tragedy ensues. Take Herodias and her daughter, for example. They viewed John the Baptist as a pest, and they schemed to have him murdered and his head brought to them on a platter. Today they're remembered in history as villains. Their evil schemes came from their mistaken thoughts, and their thoughts arose from their wicked hearts.

That's why the Bible says, "To be carnally minded is death, but to be spiritually minded is life and peace" (Romans 8:6). We only gain wisdom when Jesus Christ is at the very center of our heart and mind.

And He said to me, "My grace is sufficient for you, for My strength is made perfect in weakness." Therefore most gladly I will rather boast in my infirmities, that the power of Christ may rest upon me.
2 CORINTHIANS 12:9

The American Heritage Dictionary defines a *paradox* as "a statement that seems to contradict itself but may nonetheless be true." And the New Testament gives us several good examples: We receive by giving; we live by dying; we become great by becoming small, and more.

One of the most important paradoxes for Christian living is found in the apostle Paul's experience with weakness and strength. When he found himself to be weak, he asked God to remove the weakness so he could once again be strong enough to serve. But instead of removing the weakness, God gave Paul grace to experience the strength and power of Jesus Christ in his life. It was when Paul was willing to be humanly weak that he was in the right place to experience the strength of Christ. And therein lies the paradox: We become strong (in Christ) as we recognize our own human weakness, when we depend more on Him and less on ourselves.

Today: Rise early; exercise; eat healthy; sleep well. But remember that your true strength is the strength of Jesus.

Then [Jesus] took the child by the hand, and said to her, "Talitha, cumi,"
which is translated, "Little girl, I say to you, arise."

MARK 5:41

Bethesda, Maryland, took its name from a church called the
Bethesda Meeting House (1820), which took its name from
the Pool of Bethesda in Jerusalem. In Hebrew, *bet hesed* meant
"house of kindness/mercy." It is not surprising that one of
America's largest centers of healing, Walter Reed National
Military Medical Center, is located in Bethesda.

It was at the Pool of Bethesda where the sick in Jesus' day
gathered to look for healing when an angel stirred the waters.
And it was there that Jesus chose to heal a very sick man—he
was an invalid for 38 years (John 5:1-15). There is no mention of
why Jesus chose to heal this man, nor why He didn't heal others
that day. Jesus didn't heal every sick person he met. But those
He did heal were truly healed—body, soul, and spirit. Like the
young girl who had died in Capernaum whom Jesus restored
to life with a word. Healing is never a question of God's ability,
but of His purpose.

God's healing is always a gift of kindness and mercy. Ask if
you are in need, and trust Him for His answer.

FEBRUARY 23
Darkness

I am distraught.
PSALM 88:15

Psalm 88 is the saddest of the Psalms. Many Psalms are happy and exuberant, like Psalm 100 and 103. Some begin on a low note but end on a more hopeful frame of mind, such as Psalm 130. Only one Psalm begins on a low note and ends in the same place—Psalm 88. The writer, Heman, was distraught, and his final words were "darkness is my closest friend" (verse 18, NIV).

But Heman never gave up. He did the one thing he *could* do—he prayed. Every verse is a prayer, and Heman never yielded to despair. He simply kept praying. Sometimes that's all we can do—and the most important thing we can ever do. When we face confusion and doubt, we have the full authority of our Sovereign Lord to help us win the battle. We can be overcomers through Him. Even amid prolonged low spirits, we can maintain the lifeline of prayer.

And we can remember that the next Psalm begins with the words: "I will sing of the mercies of the Lord forever" (Psalm 89:1).

*You, O Lord, are a shield for me, my glory and
the One who lifts up my head.*

PSALM 3:3

When the apostle Paul told us to take up the shield of faith
(Ephesians 6:16), he was harkening back to the Psalms, where
God is likened to a shield around us. Psalm 5:12 says that God
surrounds us with favor as with a shield. Psalm 18:30 says, "The
word of the Lord is proven; He is a shield to all who trust in
Him." Psalm 28:7 says, "The Lord is my strength and my shield;
my heart trusted in Him, and I am helped."

Satan's destructive missiles cannot penetrate the presence
of God around us or the promises of God available to us. When
you acknowledge Christ as your Lord and become a recipient of
His grace, Satan cannot gain the victory over you. The darts of
Satan cannot pierce our protective shield of faith.

If you feel under attack, remember the truth of verses like
Psalm 84:11: "For the Lord God is a sun and shield; the Lord
will give grace and glory; no good thing will He withhold from
those who walk uprightly."

FEBRUARY 29
Know More, Trust More

That I may know Him and the power of His resurrection, and the
fellowship of His sufferings, being conformed to His death.
PHILIPPIANS 3:10

Imagine you have your toddlers with you on a shopping trip and you need to dash into a store. So you ask a stranger, "Would you mind watching my children while I run in this store?" Now imagine your best friend is with you and you leave the children with him or her. To which person would you entrust your children?

Trust (faith) in a relationship comes with knowledge over time—it is a relationship that has been tested and proven in the past allowing for faith in the present. The Bible is filled with references to knowing God, and time is almost always part of the context. Knowledge, and therefore trust, grows over time. Paul prayed that God would give the Ephesians "knowledge of Him" (Ephesians 1:17) and that they would grow into unity in the "knowledge of the Son of God" (Ephesians 4:13). Both verses suggest that time is a factor.

Don't be discouraged if you feel you lack faith. Instead, seek to know God better. The more you know Him, the more you will trust Him. And that takes time with Him and in His Word.

MARCH

MARCH 1
God and You

Then Elijah said to the people, "I alone am left a prophet of the Lord; but Baal's prophets are four hundred and fifty men."

1 KINGS 18:22

There is an old saying: "God plus one is a majority." God is eternal and infinite; God is the Creator of us all. Even if all the 7.7 billion souls on earth stood against God, He would still be bigger.

That must have been Elijah's mindset when he met the prophets of Baal on Mount Carmel. It was 450 prophets of Baal against Elijah and his God, yet Elijah was still in the majority. He had no hesitation in standing for God against a crowd of hundreds who were arrayed against Him. Therein lies the test of faith: Can we see ourselves in the majority when the forces of life are stacked against us—either people or circumstances? Elijah needed God to show up and demonstrate His power to convince the Baal worshipers that their idol was impotent and God was all-powerful. Elijah asked for God to manifest His greatness, and He did. And the prophets of Baal—the true minority—fled and were destroyed.

Don't hesitate to ask God to be with you against the world. With God, all things are possible.

Over everything the glory will be a canopy.
ISAIAH 4:5, NIV

Throughout the Bible, storms are illustrations of the hardships of life, yet we are constantly told of Him who is our shelter in the storm. One especially vivid passage is found in Isaiah 4, which describes the city of Jerusalem during the coming Millennial reign of Christ. Verses 5-6 say, "Then the Lord will create over all of Mount Zion ... a cloud of smoke by day and a glow of flaming fire by night; over everything the glory will be a canopy. It will be a shelter and shade from the heat of the day, and a refuge and hiding place from the storm and rain" (NIV).

While this is talking about the city of Jerusalem during the future Millennium, there is an unmistakable application for God's people now. The presence of your God envelops you. His glory covers you like a cloud by day and a fire by night. Visualize His closeness and think of Him in that way. His presence will brighten the dark days, and His canopy of blessings will be a hiding place from the storm and rain.

Watch, stand fast in the faith, be brave, be strong.
1 CORINTHIANS 16:13

Who needs body armor? Not just military personnel and police officers. An organization called Vested Interest in K9s is suiting up America's 30,000 police dogs in protective gear. Each ballistic suit can cost up to $2,000, and the charity has cloaked more than 2,900 four-legged warriors since 2009.

As believers, we too have a vested interest in protecting ourselves from Satan's ballistic attacks. One unguarded moment can ruin our testimonies, damage our relationships, diminish our influence, steal our joy, and reverse our spiritual progress.

We have power available to be overcomers in life, with God's armor and the Holy Spirit to protect and guide us. In the final verses of 1 Corinthians, the apostle Paul told us to keep alert for spiritual danger (watch); to hold our convictions tightly (stand fast in the faith); to exercise courage (be brave); and to draw energy from God for our daily battles with the world, the flesh, and the devil (be strong).

Anything else and you're barking up the wrong tree.

Let your speech always be with grace, seasoned with salt,
that you may know how you ought to answer each one.
COLOSSIANS 4:6

One summer while staying in a vacation cottage, Rich DeVos noticed the garbage collector making his rounds. This man showed up precisely at 6:30 a.m. once a week, moving from cottage to cottage carefully so as not to awaken people. The man was graceful in how he stashed the garbage in his vehicle, and he kept the neighborhood tidy. One morning, DeVos went out and told him, "You're doing a great job. I came out to tell you that I really appreciate the good job you're doing." The man replied that in twelve years of hauling garbage, no one had ever said a kind word to him, including his boss.[3]

Great communicators don't just give speeches or deliver sermons. They know how to say a kind word to those they meet along the way. Today you can say a kind word to someone who hasn't heard one for a while. A kind word is never wasted.

[3] Rich DeVos, *Hope From My Heart* (Nashville: J Countryman, 2000), 58-59.

MARCH 9

Redeem the Time

Send Zenas the lawyer and Apollos on their journey with haste.
TITUS 3:13

At the close of a busy day, have you ever sat down and wondered where the day went? Or the week? Or even the month? Our busy lives contribute to the feeling that time is quickly passing by. How do we slow things down? By taking time for things of the Lord. The Lord hasn't allocated us much time on earth; we're made for eternity in heaven. In the time we have left, let's set about our Father's business with haste.

The apostle Paul wrote to Titus, giving him a message for two men—Zenas and Apollos. Of Zenas, we know nothing; he is mentioned only here in the Bible. Apollos, however, was a well-known teacher. Paul's message to them both was: There's no time to waste. Hurry up. Make haste.

Charles Spurgeon once preached a sermon from Luke 14:23, the passage where the master says to the servant, "Go out into the highways and hedges, and compel them to come in." Spurgeon was so overcome by the urgency of the task that he skipped the introduction of his sermon and started compelling people to come to Christ, immediately, urgently, now.

Let's do the same! Make haste. Time is short—eternity is waiting.

Behold, God is my salvation, I will trust and not be afraid; "for Yah, the Lord, is my strength and song; He also has become my salvation." Therefore with joy you will draw water from the wells of salvation.

ISAIAH 12:2-3

Do you ever flip to the back of a book to find out the ending? Perhaps you are hoping to discover if the main character survives a life-threatening surgery or if the love story has a happy ending? Reading the end of a story can bring peace to the reading journey, even though the exact unfolding of the events is unknown.

When we come to Christ, the end of our story is written and secure. Salvation is both deliverance from the penalty of sin and an open invitation into the presence of God for eternity and today. Regardless of the circumstances of this moment and any discouragement weighing you down, the well of salvation is deep. We can approach God with joy to receive the strength and song of Christ's sacrifice and affection. Nothing can snatch us from His hand.

Assuredly, I say to you, among those born of women there has not risen one greater than John the Baptist; but he who is least in the kingdom of heaven is greater than he.
MATTHEW 11:11

Starting in 1927, *Time* magazine began choosing a "Man of the Year." In 1999 they switched the designation to "Person of the Year." Not always an individual, the magazine has honored couples, classes, movements, and groups of people—whatever was deemed to have been the greatest influence for the preceding year.

Around A.D. 31, the choice would have been easy: John the Baptist. Jesus said that none born of women had risen greater than John the Baptist, and then He went on to state that those who are born anew into the Kingdom of God would surpass even John in greatness. What made Jesus give John the Baptist this commendation? We can speculate that John's dedication, sacrifice, commitment to calling, humility, and understanding of who Jesus was would have played a role. Many did not fully comprehend who Jesus was, but John did. He prepared the way for the ministry of Jesus, explaining to others that "'I am not the Christ,' but 'I have been sent before Him'" (John 3:28).

He said of Jesus, "He must increase, but I must decrease" (John 3:30). John knew his role and responsibility; he is a model of greatness for us all to follow.

Recognizing Jesus

Is this not the carpenter, the Son of Mary, and brother of James, Joses, Judas, and Simon? And are not His sisters here with us?

MARK 6:3

The Nicene Creed grew out of the first of seven ecumenical church councils—the First Council of Nicaea in A.D. 325. The central issue the council was tasked with debating was the nature of Jesus Christ and His relationship to God the Father. That is, was Christ truly divine? (The Council recognized that He was and is.)

A similar question evolved in Nazareth when Jesus arrived there with His disciples. His teaching in the synagogue was so profound that "many hearing Him were astonished" (Mark 6:2). Those who heard Jesus teach and saw His miracles wondered how a mere human could do such things. After all, He was from a local family—the crowds knew His mother and brothers and sisters (verse 3). They had not yet realized that Jesus was the divine Messiah of Israel—the Son of God as well as Son of Man.

While His neighbors and even His family did not fully comprehend who Jesus was, we know and affirm that Christ is the Son of God and that because He is divine, He could state: "Anyone who has seen me has seen the Father" (John 14:9, NIV).

MARCH 13
Staying Focused

Do not be wise in your own eyes; fear the Lord and depart from evil.
PROVERBS 3:7

First of all, focus is a matter of sight. We focus on the eye chart at the doctor's office; we focus our binoculars when looking at distant objects; we focus our camera lens when we take a picture.

It is not surprising that Proverbs encourages us not to "be wise in [our] own eyes." Said another way, don't trust your own eyes as a source of focus in life. There is a lot to see in this world, and much to focus on. The challenge is to make sure we are focusing on God first and seeing life through His "eyes." Proverbs 3:5 says the same thing: Trust in God with all your heart and don't lean on your own understanding. Our eyes and our understanding are gifts of God, but in a fallen world we need to constantly measure our focus against God's standards and values to make sure we are seeing, and acting, in a godly way. And that takes discipline—the discipline of submitting every thought to Christ (2 Corinthians 10:5-6).

Godly focus is a lifestyle choice. One that says, "Lord, grant me discernment and discipline to value what You value and choose what You choose."

Peace Always

May the Lord of peace Himself give you peace always
in every way. The Lord be with you all.
2 THESSALONIANS 3:16

Thomas Watson wrote, "If God be our God, He will give us peace in trouble. When there is a storm without, He will make peace within. The world can create trouble in peace, but God can create peace in trouble."

Paul ended his letters to the Thessalonians with a massive statement about peace, saying: (1) God is the Lord of peace. He possesses total peace within Himself and controls the flow and force of peace. (2) He *Himself* is peace. It's one of His attributes. (3) He *gives* peace. It comes from nowhere else. (4) He gives peace *always*. There's no circumstance in life beyond His ability to provide inner peace. (5) He gives peace *in every way*. It's hard to comprehend all that means, but it surely involves our spirit, soul, mind, and emotions. (6) His peace is accompanied by His presence—"the Lord be *with you all*."

This world is full of distractions, distresses, and disasters. But there is a place of peace—it is in Him, and it *is* Him!

MARCH 15
Peter the Impulsive

Then Peter took [Jesus] aside and began to rebuke Him, saying,
"Far be it from You, Lord; this shall not happen to You!"
MATTHEW 16:22

In terms of human strengths and weaknesses, many counselors hold the view that weaknesses are simply strengths misused or over-applied. Or, a weakness is an immature expression of a strength. For example, impulsivity, speaking without thinking, and hyperactivity might mellow into enthusiasm, boldness, and proactivity. That might have been the case with the apostle Peter.

Peter is a favorite disciple of many Christians, though he suffered from a continuing case of foot-in-mouth disease from speaking without thinking. For instance, when Jesus told His disciples He would be killed in Jerusalem, Peter immediately rebuked Him: Not going to happen, Lord! Instead of asking for an explanation, Peter assumed he knew better. And when Jesus predicted Peter would deny Him three times, Peter insisted—twice—that he would never deny or disown the Lord. Impulsive? Yes. But then Peter became the epitome of boldness in the early chapters of Acts.

Maturity takes time; the fruit of the Spirit is evidence of God's conforming us to the image of Christ. Today's weakness can become tomorrow's strength.

MARCH 16
His Healing Touch

[The Servant of the Lord] has no form or comeliness; and when
we see Him, there is no beauty that we should desire Him.

ISAIAH 53:2

If you had lived in the first century, would you have recognized Jesus as the Messiah—Isaiah's Servant of the Lord? Isaiah compared Him to a scrubby plant growing up in the parched landscape of Judea (53:2). On a dusty road you likely wouldn't have given Him a second look. His clothes were typical of the day: plain and serviceable.

Yet when a sick woman reached out in a crowd and touched the hem of Jesus' cloak, she was healed. Was there some power in Jesus' garments? No—Jesus said it was her faith that resulted in her healing (Mark 5:34). Too often we put faith in the outward appearance, but God looks at the heart (1 Samuel 16:7). It was Jesus' identity as the Son of God that brought healing, not His position or prominence or appearance.

The lesson for us is the same: It is what God has done in our lives that can help others. It doesn't matter if we lack the riches of the world. God has given us the riches of His kingdom—it's all we need to bring help and healing to others (Luke 12:32).

MARCH 17
Save Some

By all means save some.
1 CORINTHIANS 9:22

The average person spends more than five years of his or her life on social media, and the average teen spends 9 hours a day using social media.[4] To appreciate the generational shift that is occurring, consider this: People older than 50 spend 50 hours a week watching television, but people between 25 and 34 watch a "mere" 26.5 hours a week. They're looking at smaller screens instead.[5]

None of us can afford to give that much time to social media. Turn over a new leaf today and consider how to reduce the time you and your children spend online. Reduce the number of apps you use. Adopt more productive hobbies so you'll have less time to waste.

But when you *are* on social media sites, think of 1 Corinthians 9:22, where Paul said he used "all means" to share Christ. We have new platforms now for quoting Scripture, for testifying, for pointing others to the Lord. We can share insights and links that advance the Kingdom.

Turn your social media into social ministry, and let's use "all means" to save some.

---

[4] https://www.entrepreneur.com/slideshow/306136
[5] https://www.nytimes.com/2016/07/01/business/media/nielsen-survey-media-viewing.html

MARCH 22
Forgiveness

*When Jesus saw [the friends'] faith, He said to the
paralytic, "Son, your sins are forgiven you."*
MARK 2:5

The hardest part of forgiving another person is *acting like
the offense never occurred*. But that is what forgiving someone
means—restoring relationships to the status they enjoyed
before the offense took place. It's one thing to say, "I forgive
you," but it's another to act like all the effects of an offense are
completely erased. After all, according to Paul in 1 Corinthians
13, love is known by its actions more than its words.

Jesus faced this dilemma when He healed a paralytic man.
When He told the man that his sins were forgiven (and by
extension, he was healed), He was criticized. He was accused
of blaspheming by saying He had the authority to forgive
sins—something only God can do. So, Jesus proved He had the
authority to say, "I forgive you," by doing something harder. He
healed the man's paralysis. After all, as Jesus explained, actions
speak louder than words (Mark 2:8-11).

We cannot go through life without being hurt by others,
so we should learn to forgive. Even more, we should practice
demonstrating our forgiveness by our acts of lovingkindness.
Look for opportunities to do both.

Don't Forget to Pray

Where shall we buy bread, that these may eat?
JOHN 6:5

Because of his faithful work with orphans, George Müller is considered a hero in the faith. But his ministry nearly ended before it began because he forgot to pray about something. Müller had prayed for all aspects of his envisioned orphan house—land, building, supplies, provisions. "There was, however, one point I never had prayed about, namely that the Lord would send children; for I naturally took it for granted that there would be plenty of applications." The work began without any children! Müller went back to his knees, and the next day the first application for the orphanage arrived.

God's provisions come in response to our prayers. In John 6, Phillip asked Jesus how to feed the five thousand; and Jesus, of course, was waiting to be asked for He knew exactly what He was planning to do. He is not limited by our obstacles.

Müller said, "In leaning upon the living God alone, we are beyond disappointment, and beyond being forsaken .... How precious to know that surely no good thing shall be withheld from us whilst we walk uprightly!"

Your God will meet your needs. Trust Him today.

MARCH 24
A Song of Praise

And Miriam answered them: "Sing to the Lord,
for He has triumphed gloriously!"
EXODUS 15:21

We first meet Miriam in Exodus 2 when she was a child on the banks of the River Nile watching her baby brother's voyage in a basket. We next see her in Exodus 15, an aged woman on the shores of the Red Sea, joining her brother in joyful praises of thanksgiving for Israel's deliverance. Miriam is the first soloist in the history of hymnody. As the Israelites realized God had miraculously saved them at the Red Sea, someone hastily wrote a hymn of praise, which is the first recorded song in the Bible (Exodus 15:1-19). The assembly sang it. "Then Miriam the prophetess, the sister of Aaron, took the timbrel in her hand; and all the women went out after her with timbrels and with dances. And Miriam answered them: 'Sing to the Lord'" (Exodus 15:20-21).

Like Miriam, we have our share of difficulty and danger, but a thankful spirit keeps us praising Him who makes a way when there seems to be no way. From childhood to old age, we should sing our thanksgivings to the Lord, for He has triumphed gloriously!

> *Yet Michael the archangel, in contending with the devil, when*
> *he disputed about the body of Moses, dared not bring against*
> *him a reviling accusation, but said, "The Lord rebuke you!"*
> JUDE 1:9

In northwest Russia, where the Northern Dvina River empties into the White Sea, sits the city of Archangel (Russian *Arkhangelsk*). The city took its name from the Michael the Archangel Monastery that is located there.

Michael is one of only two angels whose names are given to us in Scripture—the other being Gabriel. And Michael is the only one of the two called "archangel" (though Gabriel is referred to as such in the non-biblical book of Enoch). *Arch* comes from the Greek word meaning "to rule," so an archangel can be understood as a ruling, or a powerful, angel. Gabriel appears four times in Scripture, bringing messages to Daniel (twice), Zacharias (father of John the Baptist), and Mary (mother of Jesus). Michael appears to have had an overseeing role with the Jewish people (Daniel 12:1; Jude 1:9). In both cases, their faithfulness stands out.

Messengers (angels) are stewards of their messages, and stewards must be found faithful (1 Corinthians 4:2). May we be faithful stewards to deliver the Gospel of God to those who need His love and comfort.

MARCH 30
Pleasing God

This is My beloved Son, in whom I am well pleased. Hear Him!
MATTHEW 17:5

Who do you most want to please? Your spouse? Your parents? A teacher or coach? When we admire someone, we want to please them. Jesus said, "The Father has not left Me alone, for I always do those things that please Him" (John 8:29).

Just as Jesus desired to please His Father, we should seek to please Jesus. The book of Hebrews gives us two specific ways of pleasing Him. First, He is pleased when we trust Him with our burdens and exercise faith in Him. Hebrews 11 says, "By faith Enoch was taken away so that he did not see death, 'and was not found, because God had taken him'; for before he was taken he had this testimony, that he pleased God. But without faith it is impossible to please Him" (verses 5-6).

Second, according to Hebrews 13, the Lord is pleased when we are generous and share with those in need: "But do not forget to do good and to share, for with such sacrifices God is well pleased" (verse 16).

Is there something you need to commit to God in faith? Is there someone who needs your act of kindness today? Make the decision to please God with your actions today.

MARCH 31
Blazing Truth

Is not My word like a fire?
JEREMIAH 23:29

In *The Pilgrim's Progress*, the character named Interpreter showed Christian a large fire burning against a wall with a roaring flame. A man was throwing water on the fire, trying to quench the flame. Yet the fire blazed all the greater. Christian asked, "What means this?" Interpreter explained that the devil stands in front of us trying to quench our flame for Christ; but then he led Christian behind the wall where a man with a supply of oil was secretly and constantly feeding the fire.

A lot of things can happen today to quench our motivation and morale, but we have a secret fuel constantly being piped into our hearts by the Holy Spirit—the flammable Word of God. In Jeremiah 20, the prophet Jeremiah grew discouraged and said, "I am in derision daily; everyone mocks me" (verse 7). He wanted to give up, but he went on to say, "But His word was in my heart like a burning fire shut up in my bones; I was weary of holding it back, and I could not" (verse 9).

Make sure your heart is always blazing with fresh truths from God's Word.

APRIL

APRIL 1
Generosity

And God is able to make all grace abound toward you,
that you, always having all sufficiency in all things,
may have an abundance for every good work.
2 CORINTHIANS 9:8

For many years, analyses have shown that middle- and low-income people tend to give a greater percentage of their income to charity than high-income people do. The difference isn't huge—three-plus percent to charity for middle-/low-income families, one-plus percent for high earners. It seems the more we have, the less we are willing to part with it.

Jesus made a point of praising people who gave sacrificially instead of giving out of their abundance (Mark 12:41-44). And Paul praised the Macedonian churches who gave out of their poverty to help the church in Jerusalem (2 Corinthians 8:1-4). Behind every instance of sacrificial giving is the promise that God's grace will provide "sufficiency in all things." Because giving is God-like, God's abundance undergirds it.

Giving sacrificially and generously is a way to grow faith. God can't fill a hand that has a tight grasp on money. God moves money into and out of open hands.

APRIL 6
Angelic Mysteries

Praise the Lord! Praise the Lord from the heavens; praise Him in the heights! Praise Him, all His angels; praise Him, all His hosts!
PSALM 148:1-2

We regularly learn about the discovery of an entirely new species of plant or animal found somewhere on the planet—often in the depths of the ocean or the heart of a jungle. When that happens, it reminds us of the mysteries of God's creation over which we have been made stewards.

As well as mysteries on earth, there are mysteries in the heavens. Not complete mysteries, for we have been given glimpses in Scripture of what lies beyond our sight. Angels fall into the category of "known," but not "well known." Angels exist for sure—they are mentioned nearly three hundred times in the Bible. But they are invisible to us (Jacob saw angels in a dream, but not while awake—Genesis 28:12), yet apparently all around us (Psalm 103:20; Hebrews 1:14). All appear to have been originally loyal to God, but some rebelled and fell from His presence (Matthew 25:41; Revelation 12:9). They are invisible to us but innumerable before God (Revelation 5:11).

Someday all mysteries will be revealed. Until then, glory today in the wondrous works of God—including His angels.

APRIL 7

Joy—the Business of Heaven

My heart rejoices in the Lord.
1 SAMUEL 2:1

In the book of Philippians, the apostle Paul said, "Finally, my brethren, rejoice in the Lord" (3:1). He also wrote, "Rejoice in the Lord always. Again I will say, rejoice!" (4:4) These are the only times that phrase occurs in the New Testament. Paul, who loved his "books" and "parchments" was quoting from the prayer of an Old Testament hero—Hannah. In 1 Samuel 1, Hannah was distraught beyond comfort, being tormented by her circumstances. Going to the tabernacle in Shiloh, Hannah earnestly prayed over her situation, and God graciously answered. In chapter 2, she composed a rich hymn of thanksgiving, which began with the words Paul later used to encourage the Philippians: "Rejoice in the Lord."

Hannah teaches us that our expressions of joyful thanksgiving reverberate through history. When we exhibit a thankful attitude, it's transmitted to others; through them it reaches even more people. Our attitudes are passed down through the generations. If we're angry or depressed or sullen or anxious, our children will absorb those attitudes. But when we approach life with a joyful spirit of thanksgiving, it leaves a lasting legacy.

So rejoice in the Lord always. And again I say: Rejoice!

APRIL 8

A Good Man's Steps

The steps of a good man are ordered by the Lord, and He delights in his way.

PSALM 37:23

Being a follower of Christ is delightful. Psalm 37:4 tells us to delight ourselves in the Lord, and He will give us the desires of our heart. The psalmist said, "I delight to do Your will, O my God" (Psalm 40:8). We're to delight in His Word day and night, to delight ourselves in His statutes (Psalm 1:2; Psalm 119:16). Our heart finds delight in the ways of the Lord (2 Chronicles 17:6) and in the abundance of peace (Psalm 37:11). We delight in doing His will (Psalm 40:8).

The best part, however, is knowing that, incredibly, the Lord delights in us! The psalmist said, "He also brought me out into a broad place; He delivered me because He delighted in me" (Psalm 18:19). Proverbs 15:8 says that God delights in the prayers of the upright. First Kings 10:9 says, "Blessed be the Lord your God, who delighted in you."

Delighting in the Lord puts the worries of life into perspective. We should begin each day with the euphoria of God's joy and end each day with the assurance of God's presence.

How wonderful to live such a life!

APRIL 9
Man of Sorrows

Rachel died and was buried on the way to Ephrath (that is, Bethlehem).
GENESIS 35:19

The thread of redemptive history winds through Bethlehem, and the story begins in the book of Genesis. One of Scripture's greatest love stories ended when Jacob's beloved wife, Rachel, died during childbirth and was buried in Bethlehem. Genesis 35:16-20 gives us: (1) the longest account of the death of a woman in the Bible; (2) the story of the first woman in Scripture to die during childbirth; (3) the first occurrence of the word "grave" in the Bible when referring to death; and (4) the first time in Scripture a gravestone was erected.

But there's more. With her dying words, Rachel named her son, Ben-Oni, which means, "Son of My Sorrow." But Jacob renamed the boy Benjamin, which means, "Son of the Right Hand."

Think of it. A Man of Sorrows, born in Bethlehem, who came to dwell at the right hand of his beloved Father. As early as Genesis 35, we have inklings of our Lord's own story—nearly two thousand years before He came. The whole Bible is about Jesus! You can trust a Book like that, and you can trust the Savior of whom it speaks.

APRIL 18
Going With the Flow

My sheep hear My voice, and I know them and they follow Me.
JOHN 10:27

In the Summer Olympic sport of kayaking, contestants mostly go with the current, navigating through gates. At times they are asked to reverse course, paddle against the whitewater current, go through the gate, then reverse direction back into the mainstream current. Going *with* the current is easier than going *against* the current.

The same is true in the Christian life. James 4:6 says that God gives grace to the humble but resists the proud. Humility is going with God's "current" while pride is resisting His "current." Think of God's role as a shepherd of His sheep. One of a shepherd's responsibilities is to lead his sheep. Following the shepherd is to go with the flow; going one's own way is to risk danger. The Bible is filled with images of God as a shepherd who leads His sheep. Contented, peaceful sheep are those who follow God into places of rest and provision.

When life gets challenging, check to see if you are following God or not. Even if He leads us into a storm, as long as He is there we can be at rest (Mark 4:37-41).

APRIL 19
Trust and Wait

Wait on the Lord; be of good courage, and He shall strengthen your heart; wait, I say, on the Lord!

PSALM 27:14

We wait a year for a birthday or an anniversary. We wait nine months for babies to be born. We wait days to attend a sporting event. We wait minutes for a taxi to arrive. In all that waiting, we rarely wait anxiously because we are usually confident in the outcome. The baby will be born, the game will begin, the taxi will arrive, the celebration will be held. Certainty of outcome can make the difference in how we wait.

In life, sometimes we are anxious about the future because we aren't certain of what it holds. And we too often wait anxiously; our heart grows weak with uncertainty and fear. But God knows the future; indeed, His knowledge is unlimited. We may not know the future, but we know Who does. Therefore, we have every reason to wait with courage, certainty, and confidence. God promises to give courage and strength to those who wait upon Him.

Are you looking to the future, unsure of what it holds? Trust in the Lord (Proverbs 3:5-6). Receive His strength for your heart as you wait upon Him.

APRIL 20
Deciding to Serve God

As for me and my house, we will serve the Lord.
JOSHUA 24:15

Eat at a build-your-own sandwich, salad, burrito or pizza restaurant, and you quickly learn how many choices a human being can make in a short amount of time. From the type of bread or crust, to rice or beans, to pepperoni or olives, there are a lot of decisions! But when it comes to how we live our life, we must continually make the same decision—to serve God.

As believers we are confronted with the choice to obey and serve God or to disregard His Word and live for ourselves multiple times each day. Peace versus anger. Kindness versus animosity. Truth versus falsehood. However, like the Israelites in the time of Joshua, we can have direction and purpose each time we are confronted with one of these choices by purposing each day to serve the Lord. The God who has asked us to serve Him has given us all that we have and has made us all that we are, so how can we not help but choose to serve Him each day of our life.

But when He saw the multitudes, He was moved with compassion for them,
because they were weary and scattered, like sheep having no shepherd.

MATTHEW 9:36

The northwest part of England—the so-called "hill country"—
is sheep country. A stranger traveling in those parts might
wonder at the large number of sheep grazing seemingly
unattended, on the rugged fells (hills). But a closer look will
reveal miles of dry-stone walls that provide boundaries to
their grazing, and color markings that indicate their owner.
Hill-country sheep do not lack for a shepherd; they are far too
valuable.

And so are the people of God whom the Bible calls sheep.
As Jesus moved throughout the towns of Israel, preaching
and ministering, He saw people who seemed to be wandering
through life without a divine Shepherd. And "He was moved
with compassion for them, because they were weary and
scattered" (Matthew 9:36). These were the very people He
came into the world to save, people who were disconnected
from the love of God. And Jesus' compassion prompted Him to
action—He raised up workers to take His reconciling Gospel
into the world.

Let your love manifest itself in compassion and let
compassion result in action on behalf of those in need.

*Now when all the people saw it, they fell on their faces; and
they said, "The Lord, He is God! The Lord, He is God!"*
1 KINGS 18:39

Christian apologist Josh McDowell published his first major
book in 1972—*Evidence That Demands a Verdict*. It was a
compendium of evidence supporting the trustworthiness of the
Bible and the authenticity of its message about Jesus Christ.

Any courtroom judge will tell you: Evidence demands a
verdict! We face evidence every day in a variety of matters;
every decision (verdict) we render in life is based on evidence
of some kind. When we encounter the evidence for the reality
of the God of the Bible, we are called upon to make a decision.
As Jesus asked His disciples, "Who do you say that I am?" (Luke
9:20) Evidence demands a verdict. And the evidence God
presented of His power and reality on Mount Carmel caused all
the people of Israel to shout, "The Lord, He is God!" Many of
them had been following Baal, but the evidence of God's power
through Elijah changed their minds.

The more you study the Bible, the more evidence you will
have that God can meet every need. Let Him prove Himself to
you (Malachi 3:10).

Then [Jesus] went up into the boat to them, and the wind ceased. And they were greatly amazed in themselves beyond measure, and marveled.

MARK 6:51

A time loop is used by film directors as a way to have a character repeat and re-experience a moment in time. One of the most well-known films of this genre was the 1993 comedy *Groundhog Day* in which a TV reporter repeated the same day over and over and over.

Sometimes it seems Jesus' disciples started out each day with no memory of lessons learned. For example, they witnessed Jesus feeding a crowd of many thousands with only five loaves of bread and two fish (Mark 6:30-44). In other words, they had witnessed Jesus doing an amazing miracle! Then, just a few hours later, with the miracle fresh in their memories, they witnessed Jesus walking on the water of the Sea of Galilee and "cried out" and "were troubled" (Mark 6:49-50). In other words, they didn't connect one miracle with another; each new miracle brought a "Who is this?" response from them.

We must treasure everything God does for us, big or small, building miracle memory. Not only will it lessen our surprise, but it will also increase our faith.

Persevere

Tribulation produces perseverance; and perseverance,
character; and character, hope.
ROMANS 5:3-4

Recently a student was asked to give a talk at his church, and he spoke of the importance of perseverance, but he didn't know how to correctly pronounce that word. Throughout his talk, he kept talking about *presseverance*. His listeners smiled and nodded in agreement because they fully understood that perseverance really is press-everance. It's the quality of pressing forward whatever comes.

We demonstrate our integrity when we stick with our commitments without wavering, even when grueling times arrive. The apostle Paul emphasized this quality over and over. He told the Romans that the quality of perseverance created hopeful hearts (Romans 5:3-4). He told the Corinthians about his own perseverance as he labored among them and faced great opposition (2 Corinthians 12:12). He told the Ephesians to be "watchful to this end with all perseverance and supplication for all the saints" (Ephesians 6:18). And he reminded Timothy, "But you have carefully followed my doctrine, manner of life, purpose, faith, longsuffering, love, perseverance" (2 Timothy 3:10).

Let's be true to our commitments to God and others as we "press toward the goal for the prize of the upward call of God in Christ Jesus" (Philippians 3:14).

Keep your heart with all diligence, for out of it spring the issues of life.
PROVERBS 4:23

Many futurists predict that clean water will become the focus of national and international attention in the years to come. As the global population grows, more clean water is polluted, along with depletion of underground aquifers. Humanitarian agencies are making strong efforts to dig wells in lands where clean water is scarce. Water is second only to oxygen on the list of human necessities.

It is not surprising that in the arid biblical lands water and its sources were a frequent and potent symbol of health and vitality. The father in the book of Proverbs told his son to guard his heart carefully, "for from it flow the springs of life" (Proverbs 4:23, NASB). The heart is like a deep well from which flow "the issues of life" (NKJV). "Everything you do flows from [the heart]" (NIV). Just as a poisoned well can put an end to physical life, so a defiled heart can sicken the spiritual life (Mark 7:14-23).

What efforts are you making to protect the purity of the heart-spring that gives life to all you do? What filters do you have in place to screen out impurities? "Keep your heart with all diligence."

APRIL 30
Love Without Conditions

For He shall give His angels charge over you, to keep you in all your ways.
PSALM 91:11

The prodigal son was lost, not just physically removed but spiritually and relationally. He had intentionally wished his father dead and cut off communication by moving to a faraway land. When he returned, he was celebrated with abandon, generosity, and joy. As his father celebrated the restoration of his son, everyone who loved the father joined in. They knew how much the son meant to the father: They loved the son because they loved the father.

Although the older brother had never left home, his heart was in a faraway land. Instead of mirroring the father's joy, he was afraid there was not enough of the father's wealth to go around. His love for his father was replaced by the priority and love for money and what he felt he deserved.

The angels of God know better. God's power, peace, presence, and provision are infinite. In our finite minds we have difficulty grasping the height, depth, and width of God's love: It never ends. The angels in heaven celebrate every time a human being returns to God—that is how deep His love is for us.

MAY 4
First Responders

Then the secret was revealed to Daniel in a night vision.
So Daniel blessed the God of heaven.
DANIEL 2:19

Sadly, "first responders" is a term we know all too well today. They are the trained technicians who are the first on the scene of a tragedy or disaster: police, medical personnel, fire fighters, wilderness and water rescuers, various military units, humanitarian teams, and others. What is the first response of the first responders? It is to save, to help, to give aid and comfort wherever needed.

Christians might be considered "first responders" in the world as well, offering whatever practical help we can to those in need. But what about our "first response"? Paul gives three good ones in 1 Thessalonians 5:16-18: rejoice, pray, give thanks. Specifically, how often do we couple prayer and thanksgiving together? When we pray, and God answers, what is our first response? In Scripture, it is often praise before anything else. When Daniel and his three friends prayed for God's intervention in Babylon, the answer came, and Daniel's first response was to praise God (Daniel 2:17-23).

God is to be praised and thanked in all things, as Paul wrote—but especially when He answers our prayers.

MAY 5
Healing

Suddenly, a woman who had a flow of blood for twelve years
came from behind and touched the hem of His garment.
MATTHEW 9:20

Jesus healed many people in the Gospels, and He raised the
dead. But His miracles were, in a sense, temporary, for all these
people eventually died. Take the woman with the flow of blood.
She reached through the crowd and touched the edge of our
Lord's robe as He passed by. Instantly power flashed from Him,
through His garment, into her body, and she was healed. But
as time passed this woman grew old or ill, and she eventually
passed away.

Why, then, did Jesus heal the sick? To demonstrate His
power over disease. Why did He raise the dead? To exhibit His
power over death. His miracles of healing show us two things.
First, He can heal us presently, even miraculously, if and when
He chooses. Second, ultimate healing awaits us at the moment
of the Resurrection. Not a shred of death or disease will enter
heaven with us.

Jesus is the everlasting healer. He heals not only physical
afflictions but also the diseases of the soul. And our ultimate
healing is permanent, powerful, and awaiting us in eternity. By
His stripes we are healed.

MAY 6
The Better Principle

"Look!" [the king] answered, "I see four men loose, walking in the midst of the fire; and they are not hurt, and the form of the fourth is like the Son of God."

DANIEL 3:25

The "better" principle is illustrated a number of different ways in Proverbs. For instance, Proverbs 15:16 says, "Better is a little with the fear of the Lord, than great treasure with trouble." And Proverbs 16:8 reminds us that "better is a little with righteousness, than vast revenues without justice."

Another example of the "better" principle is this: Being in God's will in a difficult place is better than being out of God's will in an easy place. Or, said another way: Being in a hard place *with* God is better than being in an easy place *without* Him. There are examples in Scripture. When the three young Hebrew men found themselves in a fiery furnace in Babylon, they discovered that another person—"like the Son of God"— was with them. And they came out alive. Likewise, when the disciples were crossing the Sea of Galilee with Jesus in a storm, His presence assured their survival.

God may not always keep us out of hard places, but He is always with us. A hard place with Him is better than an easy place without Him.

MAY 7

The Woman in Your Life

Forsake foolishness and live, and go in the way of understanding.

PROVERBS 9:6

In Proverbs 9, we find a woman working hard to prepare a banquet. She starts by building a house for it, hewing out seven pillars. Then she selects the menu, prepares the feast, and sends maidens who find the highest spots in town to shout the invitations: "Come, eat of my bread and drink of the wine I have mixed" (verse 5). The woman's name is Wisdom, and Proverbs 9 describes all the blessings that come from her menu.

But the chapter ends with another woman: "A foolish woman is clamorous; she is simple, and knows nothing" (verse 13). Lady Folly also sends invitations into the streets, saying, "Whoever is simple, let him turn in here" (verse 16). Her meal is junk food that ruins the heart.

Every person on earth goes to one house or the other for their understanding of life. One or the other of these addresses is downloaded onto the GPS of your soul. You'll have a better life by going to Wisdom's address. There you can feast on the richness of God's Word, drink from the well of His thoughts, and be sustained by the energy of His Spirit.

MAY 12
Better to Obey

So Samuel said [to Saul]: "Has the Lord as great delight in burnt offerings and sacrifices, as in obeying the voice of the Lord? Behold, to obey is better than sacrifice, and to heed than the fat of rams."

1 SAMUEL 15:22

Author and pastor Ben Patterson was mountain climbing with three friends when he took an ill-advised short-cut and got separated from the others and found himself trapped on an icy ledge. When his friends finally found him, they talked him off the ledge, telling him where to put his feet (which he couldn't see) as he inched off the ledge. Only by obeying the instructions of his more-experienced friends was he saved from certain death.

There is value in obedience. Often we think we have a better idea or plan than God. But once we execute our plan we lose the opportunity of seeing how beneficial God's plan would have been. Saul, the first king of Israel, learned the hard way that God delights in obedience more than anything else. When Saul substituted his plan for God's, it cost him the throne of Israel (1 Samuel 15).

One of the greatest challenges of the Christian life is to learn that God says what He says *for a reason*. Better to take Him at His word.

Therefore He is also able to save to the uttermost those who come to God through Him, since He always lives to make intercession for them.

HEBREWS 7:25

You've seen it—in a professional sporting event two players are on the verge of tussling with one another. Before the disagreement can flare up, a referee gets between the two players and tries to push them apart. Literally speaking, that person is an intercessor—a go-between, if you will. The English *intercede* is from a Latin word of two parts: *inter* meaning "between" and *cedere* meaning "go." An intercessor is a go-between.

Jesus Christ is the intercessor for the Church and for every believer. He stands between us and the Father as our personal advocate—pleading our case. If we sin, Christ "speaks to the Father in our defense" (1 John 2:1, NIV, 1984). He declares our sins having been atoned for at the Cross. If Satan accuses us before the Father, as he accused Job (Job 1:9-11; 2:4-5), Jesus defends us (Romans 8:34) since there is "now no condemnation to those who are in Christ Jesus" (Romans 8:1).

At this very moment, the Son of God Himself is advocating for you at the throne of God. He is our divine Intercessor.

Serve the Lord without distraction.
1 CORINTHIANS 7:35

If you're traveling through the village of Mantua in northeast Ohio, don't drive with a dog in your lap. Determined to stop distracted driving, the police are aggressively issuing tickets for texting and for driving with an animal sitting on one's lap. All around the world, new laws are being written to address distracted driving. In the U.S., approximately nine people are killed and more than one thousand injured each day in crashes involving a distracted driver.

It's also important to let nothing distract us from a driving faith in Christ. Hebrews 12:1 tells us to "lay aside every weight, and the sin which so easily ensnares us, and let us run with endurance the race that is set before us." Jesus warned us that if we aren't careful, the "cares of this world and the deceitfulness of riches" can choke the work of the Word of God in our lives (Matthew 13:22).

When we live according to God's plan, nothing can distract us. Every day provides a fresh opportunity to rededicate ourselves to the Lord and live with single-minded devotion to Him.

When Jesus heard [about Lazarus' illness], He said, "This sickness is not unto death, but for the glory of God, that the Son of God may be glorified through it."

JOHN 11:4

It's a question we usually hear from children as they contemplate the death of a loved one: "Why did Grandpa have to die?" It's one of those questions that is totally reasonable yet hard to answer in childlike terms.

There are biological and biblical reasons people die. But it's a theological reason that gives us the most comfort: Death is for the glory of God and His Son, Jesus Christ. When Jesus heard that His friend Lazarus was ill, He waited several days before visiting, by which time Lazarus was dead. But it was what He said when first hearing the news of Lazarus' illness that helps us most: "This sickness is not unto death, but for the glory of God." Just as Jesus displayed God's glory by raising Lazarus from the dead, so His glory will be revealed when we are raised from the dead as well.

The promise of Scripture is that Jesus is the resurrection and the life. All who believe in Him, though they die, will live to the glory of God (John 11:25-26).

MAY 20
Promises Kept

You have kept what You promised.
2 CHRONICLES 6:15

In golf, a do-over shot is called a mulligan. And the initial stroke doesn't count on the scorecard. Oh, how we wish there were mulligans in life! Especially when it comes to broken promises—ones we made or ones that were made to us. Broken promises are painful and regrettable. We would give anything to make those promises come true.

One thing we never have to worry about with God is broken promises. The Bible is filled with testimonies of the dependability of His words to us. His words are true and eternal; they reflect His own character. After Solomon finished dedicating the temple in Jerusalem, he declared to the people that not one word of God's promises had gone unfulfilled. God had established His people in their land as He promised He would. All of God's "exceedingly great and precious promises" to us will be kept—every one (2 Peter 1:4).

Is there a promise of God to which you are clinging? Don't let go. His Word is true and sure.

MAY 21
Joy Now and Forever

You will show me the path of life; in Your presence is fullness of joy; at Your right hand are pleasures forevermore.
PSALM 16:11

Why are patients willing to endure grueling weeks of chemotherapy? Why is a young couple willing to tighten their belts and their budget for two years? Why are some members of the military willing to undertake months of taxing training? It's because of what lies ahead: physical health, freedom from debt, and achieving a goal.

The same question could be asked of the apostle Paul: Why could he write a short letter to the Philippians and mention "joy" and "rejoice" over a dozen times while incarcerated in a Roman jail? What gave him such a perspective—that it is possible to have joy and endurance in the midst of hardship? It is because we are future-focused. Our eternal life begins when we come to know God through faith in Jesus Christ (John 17:3). We are living *now* in the *future*. The joy we will know on the new earth (Revelation 21:1-4) is the joy we can know today.

If you know Christ as Lord and Savior, you have been born from above to eternal life. Let eternal pleasure bring you fullness of joy today.

MAY 30
Freedom Seekers

If you abide in My word, you are My disciples indeed. And you shall know the truth, and the truth shall make you free."
JOHN 8:31-32

Feelings are like the sea, constantly swirling and shifting, whether in small waves or monumental ones. Every sailor knows the sea can change at a moment's notice. Thankfully God's Word does not change or shift. He is unchanging, like an anchor, a rock, or secure fortress.

When we use our emotions as barometers of truth, we swing from side to side and every issue becomes a matter of personal preference and opinion. God invites us into the security and truth found in His Word. We are invited to embrace God and His Word because they bring life and freedom.

Theologian and writer Warren Wiersbe offers this truth on defeating discouragement: *The remedy for discouragement is the Word of God. When you feed your heart and mind with its truth, you regain your perspective and find renewed strength.*

God's truth sets us free from deception, discouragement, and doubt. The life of Jesus, God's Word in the flesh, reassures us that His truth brings healing and life. As we draw close to Christ and nourish our souls, minds, and hearts with His Word, we discover the freedom we crave.

MAY 31
Ready and Willing

All that the Father gives Me will come to Me, and the
one who comes to Me I will by no means cast out.

JOHN 6:37

A leper approached Jesus and said, "If You are willing, You can make me clean." Jesus touched the man, saying, "I am willing; be cleansed"—and he was healed (Mark 1:40-42).

That event is a beautiful example of the willingness of God. In fact, there are no instances of Jesus being asked to help or heal and Him answering, "I am not willing." There is a place where the Bible says God is "not willing," and that is 2 Peter 3:9. In writing about the timing of the Day of the Lord (the End of the Age), Peter says God is "longsuffering," waiting for all who will be saved to come to Him. He is "not willing that any should perish but that all should come to repentance." Said another way, God is willing for any who want to be saved to come to Him (John 6:37; 7:37). The question is never whether God *is willing* but whether man is willing.

Have you responded to God's willing invitation to come to Him?

JUNE

JUNE 1
Tell Them

Tell them what great things the Lord has done for you.
MARK 5:19

A friend of Turning Point got tired of nuisance calls on his cell phone but upon reflection decided to use the calls to practice his evangelism. If the caller is hawking credit cards, our friend replies, "I don't need another card, but I take every opportunity to share the gift of God that money can never buy. May I tell you about it?" If the caller is selling vacation rentals, the man says, "I would love to tell you about the ultimate destination in life, a home in heaven." And so forth. While the man hasn't yet led a caller to Christ, he's found several who listened to the Gospel. One salesman said, "Hey! What's going on here? You're the second person today who has told me that!"

We're living in a day when we must be creative about sharing the Gospel, both personally and through our church ministries. Our culture is changing, and while our message never changes, we need endless creativity in making sure we get the message to as many people as possible. Too many times we focus on keeping cultural traditions instead of reaching the lost wherever they are.

Jesus was nonconventional in His ministry. Let's do as He did and tell others what great things the Lord has done for us.

JUNE 6
A Lineage of Faith

You have given me the heritage of those who fear Your name.
PSALM 61:5

When Joe Tarakjian's surgery left him in a wheelchair, he kept occupied by exploring his family tree. Joe studied genealogical sites, found relatives online, and followed every lead. He learned his great-grandparents had fled genocide by traveling from Armenia to Syria, then to France and America. "It was so gratifying to meet a 90-plus-year-old relative who you never spoke to before and you hear them light up when talking about your own mother," he said.

Those who know Christ have another family tree— the lineage of people who led us to faith. We're spiritual descendants of the message of the apostles and of the Pentecost converts in the book of Acts. The testimony of Jesus has crossed the generations to reach us.

Perhaps we can't trace this spiritual lineage very far until we can inspect the archives in heaven, but maybe you know who led you to Christ. Maybe you can find out who led that person and the one before. We have two thousand years of martyrs, heroes, and servants behind us and future generations before us. What a heritage and what a blessing! Let's rejoice in that today.

JUNE 7
Heaven Is Here

*And this is eternal life, that they may know You, the only
true God, and Jesus Christ whom You have sent.*
JOHN 17:3

Eternal life is not something we receive upon our death. We receive eternal life the moment we believe in Christ. When we regard heaven as the far-off dwelling of God, we forget that He is here, in this very moment. Wherever you are as you read this devotional, God is with you. Regardless of the place you find yourself in, your intimate connection to God remains.

When we bask in the truth of His affection and presence with grateful hearts, our souls open to receive His gifts, guidance, and peace. In the same way, the apostles received these things, whether they were in a prison cell or free and surrounded by friends.

Throughout the Gospels, Jesus declared that the Kingdom of God is at hand. We welcome the Kingdom of God into our lives when we surrender to Christ's lordship and allow the Holy Spirit to indwell and guide us. God's Kingdom is available to be experienced and expressed by believers every moment of every day, even as we look forward to eternity with Him.

JUNE 8
Overcome Evil With Good

Do not be overcome by evil, but overcome evil with good.
ROMANS 12:21

The horn on your car is amoral—like the tongue, a weapon, or money, it is dependent on its owner to be used for good or bad. The auto horn has become a tool of road rage in our culture, long blasts signaling our disapproval of another driver's actions. And maybe that driver's actions were wrong. But Scripture exhorts us to overcome evil (wrongs) with good (patience, understanding) rather than with evil (anger, retaliation).

In the Old Testament, burning coals were a symbol of judgment (Psalm 11:6; 140:10). But there are gentle ways to "pass judgment" that have better outcomes as illustrated in Proverbs: harsh words stir up anger, gentle words turn away anger (15:1); a gentle word can break a bone (25:15). For that reason, Solomon advised treating enemies kindly (25:21) as a way to "heap coals of fire on his head" (25:22)—advice repeated by the apostle Paul (Romans 12:20).

Paying back evil with evil is out. So, when you feel tempted, ask God to show you something good you can do for another person. It is possible to overcome evil with good. That's how God overcomes our sin every day—with love and goodness.

JUNE 9
The Language of Heaven

The lips of the righteous know what is acceptable.
PROVERBS 10:32

Michelle Myers, an Arizona woman, had a terrific headache. She finally went to sleep, but she woke up speaking in a British accent. The *Smithsonian* Magazine reported that her language change is actually a medical condition known as Foreign Accent Syndrome (FAS). The University of Texas says this phenomenon sometimes occurs after a stroke or head trauma. One sixteen-year-old boy woke up from a coma speaking fluent Spanish.

When we have an encounter with Jesus Christ, our language changes. It's not just a matter of cleaning up our vocabulary, though that often occurs too. It's a matter of being more encouraging in what we say. Our words and how we speak them convey truth, wisdom, cheer, and grace. As we learn the Scriptures and memorize them, we quote them more often—to the edification of our hearers. We should speak wisely, cheerfully, and biblically, or not at all. The Bible says, "Let your conversation be gracious and attractive so that you will have the right response for everyone" (Colossians 4:6, NLT).

Our earthly lips begin spreading heavenly themes, as though we belonged to another land—which we do. As we speak biblically, we're speaking the language of heaven.

JULY 6
Confidence

Let us therefore come boldly to the throne of grace, that we may
obtain mercy and find grace to help in time of need.
HEBREWS 4:16

The country music star Vince Gill once gave a small concert in a high school gymnasium. While he was onstage performing, a small girl made her way up onto the stage where she ran over to her daddy—Vince Gill—who scooped her up in his arms.

That little girl was not intimidated by her father's fame, the bright lights, or the adoring crowd. She had every confidence that she was more important to her father than anything else. And she was right! That earthly illustration helps us understand the words of Hebrews 4:16—we are exhorted to come boldly, with confidence, to God's throne of grace in prayer to "obtain mercy and find grace to help in time of need." It might be easy to be intimidated by the glory of God. But He is our Father who welcomes us, His children, into His presence.

If there is a need you're reluctant to ask God to meet, go into His presence with confidence. His mercy and grace are there for the asking.

The Jews had light and gladness, joy and honor.
ESTHER 8:16

The book of Esther describes how the Jewish people faced possible annihilation in the Persian Empire. An evil mastermind named Haman forged a plan to kill the Hebrews, but God placed Esther, herself a Jew, in the palace as queen. With God's help, Esther and her kinsman Mordecai outwitted Haman, and the Jews were delivered.

Esther 8 describes the joy that filled the Jews across the empire as they heard the news. They could defend themselves, and Mordecai, their leader, was appointed prime minister of the land. The Bible says, "And in every province and city, wherever the king's command and decree came, the Jews had joy and gladness, a feast and a holiday" (Esther 8:17).

None of us want to endure seasons of anxious stress or tense uncertainty. But after we've passed through the test, our sense of release and relief is like opening the windows to fresh air. We can breathe again. By God's providence, every trial somehow returns a blessing in His time and way. Think of some of the deliverances God has given you, and let your heart be full of light and gladness, joy and honor.

I think it is right to refresh your memory as long as I live in the tent of this body, because I know that I will soon put it aside.
2 PETER 1:13-14, NIV

Peter wrote his final letter shortly before his execution. He wasn't discouraged; he was looking forward to the future. He spoke of "looking forward to these things," and "[looking] for new heavens and a new earth in which righteousness dwells" (2 Peter 3:13-14).

Life is full of hardships and heaviness. We have the promises of God to help us in difficult days, and we have the Holy Spirit within us. We have a purpose for being here—to refresh the memory of others regarding the things of the Lord. But we'll soon put aside the tent of our earthly body, and what a relief! Goodbye hardship and heaviness. Goodbye trials and troubles. Hello Jesus! Hello heaven! Hello golden streets, glorified bodies, endless days, and the fresh air of New Jerusalem!

During difficult times, the hope of eternity gives us strength. If you're prone to worry yourself to sleep each night, turn your thoughts upward and close your eyes thinking of heaven and its eternal throne.

JULY 9
Kingdoms vs. the Kingdom

*And in the days of these kings the God of heaven will set up
a kingdom which shall never be destroyed; and the kingdom shall
not be left to other people; it shall break in pieces and consume
all these kingdoms, and it shall stand forever.*

DANIEL 2:44

Besides his scientific expertise, Sir Isaac Newton (d. 1727)
was a historian. He wrote a lengthy book—*The Chronology of
Ancient Kingdoms Amended*—that outlined the chronology (rise
and fall) of six ancient kingdoms: Greek, Egyptian, Assyrian,
Babylonian and Mede, Israelite, and Persian.

We could add more kingdoms to the ones Newton wrote
about; the pages of history tell of many. There is something in
the nature of man that wants to create a kingdom and rule over
it—probably a vestige of man's commission to rule over God's
kingdom on earth (Genesis 1:28). But all such human kingdoms
have been temporary. Their failure should serve as a reminder
that a permanent, eternal Kingdom is coming—first for a
thousand years on earth (Revelation 20:1-4), then on the new
earth for eternity (Revelation 21:1-3).

Do not be discouraged at man's failed attempts to govern
himself. Instead look for the coming of the One whose
government will know no end (Isaiah 9:6-7).

JULY 14
At What Cost?

Turn us back to You, O Lord, and we will
be restored; renew our days as of old.
LAMENTATIONS 5:21

When King Tutankhamun's tomb was discovered in 1922, it instantly became a famous tourist destination with thousands of people coming every day, year after year. Carbon dioxide from the visitors' breath and all the dust they stirred up had a dulling influence on the stunning gold walls of the tomb. The site was closed for years while the Getty Conservation Institute restored the images and installed new ventilation systems and walkways. Now King Tut's tomb is open again, but when asked how much the restoration cost, the institute says it was so expensive they won't disclose the cost.

We live in a dusty world, and the devil is always breathing down our backs. It's easy to become spiritually dull and stained. Sometimes we lose the golden glow of God's energy in our hearts. We often need for Him to do as He said in Psalm 23—to restore our souls.

But we shouldn't forget the great cost that gained all our blessings for us at Calvary, for He gave us Himself.

Let Jesus revive your heart today, then thank Him for the cleansing power of His blood.

JULY 15
Perplexity or Providence

Instead of your shame you shall have double honor, and instead of confusion they shall rejoice in their portion.

ISAIAH 61:7

Novelist Jack Kerouac once said, "I had nothing to offer anybody except my own confusion." Some people stay in a constant state of confusion. Not so the followers of Christ. The Bible says, "For God is not the author of confusion but of peace" (1 Corinthians 14:33).

We live in a confused world, and sometimes we feel baffled by the battles of life. But remember, God is never confused, and He is interested in the details of your daily life. The coincidences, accidents, breaks, flukes, happenings, chance meetings, and unexpected news are really none of the above. They are the means by which God is providentially ordering your life—"for the Lord your God is bringing you into a good land—a land with brooks, streams, and deep springs gushing out into the valleys and hills" (Deuteronomy 8:7, NIV).

Follow Him with a sense of wonder and marvel at His ways and means. To you, it's perplexity. To Him, it's Providence.

JULY 24
Stand Firm

Hypocrites! You know how to discern the face of the sky,
but you cannot discern the signs of the times.
MATTHEW 16:3

Jesus called out the religious leaders of His day who asked Him to show them a sign from heaven. He rebuked them, saying they could read the signs of the weather but could not read the signs of the times (Matthew 16:1-4).

That wasn't all Jesus said about the signs of the times. When His disciples asked Him what would be the signs (indicators) of the End of the Age, He gave them many (Matthew 24; Luke 21). And the apostle Paul wrote to Timothy about the signs of godlessness in the last days prior to Christ's return—things like loving pleasure more than loving God and a long list of others (2 Timothy 3:1-5). Given the signs that Paul mentions, all of which have to do with personal character and behavior, the world seems headed for a downward crisis.

Keep your eyes on the culture and on Christ at the same time. As the one deteriorates, the nearness of the Other increases. Prepare to stand firm and faithful until the end.

If I Perish

And so I will go to the king, which is against
the law; and if I perish, I perish!
ESTHER 4:16

When we read the story of Esther, we see how God orchestrated the events in Esther's life to reveal His purpose for her—to save the Jewish people from death. But Queen Esther had to choose to follow God's plan, His purpose, for her life. Going before the king meant risking her life, but she went, saying, "If I perish, I perish!" (Esther 4:16) Esther was fully committed to accomplishing God's purpose for her life, no matter the personal cost. Through her commitment, the Jewish people were saved, and the events in the book of Esther are still celebrated today by the Jews during the Feast of Purim.

Most of us won't be placed in such a high position of leadership as Esther was; however, we all have a God-given purpose to fulfill in our life. And God will be with us just as He was with Esther. Commit today to fulfilling God's purpose for your life and watch what God does in you. God's plan for your life is better than any plan that you could ever imagine.

JULY 30
Every Little Ailment

However, our God turned the curse into a blessing.
NEHEMIAH 13:2

Nehemiah had a simple sermon for his people in the last chapter of his book. He reminded them how the Moabites had hired the false prophet, Balaam, to curse the Israelites in the days of Moses. But, he said, God turned the curse into a blessing.

Our Lord has the power to turn the bad moments of life inside out, using them for good in ways we can't imagine and may not recognize at the time. Every seasoned believer can look backward over life and recall moments of disappointment, anxiety, or grief. We can also see, or begin to see, how God reversed the current of events and began using the incident for His glory. You can always trust Him to do that.

A British churchman of an earlier age, Edward B. Pusey, wrote, "Every contradiction of [our] will … every little ailment, every petty disappointment, will, if [we] take it cheerfully, become a blessing …. So walking on earth we may be in heaven; the ill-tempers of others, the slights and rudeness of the world, ill health, the daily accidents with which God has mercifully strewed our paths, instead of ruffling or disturbing our peace, may cause the peace of God to be 'shed abroad in our hearts.'"

JULY 31
Rejoice in Our Salvation

Though now you do not see Him, yet believing, you rejoice with joy inexpressible and full of glory, receiving the end of your faith—the salvation of your souls.

1 PETER 1:8-9

The Roman Emperor Nero is remembered in history for his persecution of Christians. During his reign, many Christians died horrendous deaths and suffered greatly. The readers of 1 Peter were facing this persecution, and to help them endure, Peter reminded them of the sure promise of salvation and an eternity with Christ. This ultimate ending was cause for joy inexpressible despite their sufferings.

Like the Early Church, we can expect to suffer and be persecuted for our faith. As Peter said, "Do not think it strange concerning the fiery trial which is to try you, as though some strange thing happened to you" (1 Peter 4:12). But no matter how the world treats us, the blood of Jesus has purchased us and given us a magnificent, permanent inheritance that nothing in this world can shake (1 Peter 1:4). When we face trials because of our faith, we can rejoice in our salvation and the promise of eternity with Christ just as the early Christians did.

*Be of good courage, and He shall strengthen
your heart, all you who hope in the Lord.*

PSALM 31:24

When the woman at the well spoke of physical water, Jesus reminded her of His spiritual water. It was the only water needed to quench the thirst in her soul permanently. We are multidimensional people, living in the physical world even as we are rooted and connected to the spiritual world.

When Jesus came, He healed and addressed physical problems, but He knew physical healing was not enough. His forgiveness and spiritual renewal were of greater importance. Without them, physical healing only touches the surface. His greatest gift of forgiveness and redemption offers a rebirth: new heart, eyes, and intimate connection to God. We are made new through Him.

At times, physical healing arrives, and situations change for the better, but sometimes our situations remain the same. God is still working, inviting us closer in the spiritual realm. We can be comforted, lifted, and healed from within, even when nothing in our physical situation changes. Whether God is saying "Yes," "Wait," or "Not yet" to your prayers, you can trust that His compassion and power are working on your behalf.

AUGUST 5
Never Alone

For He Himself has said, "I will never leave you nor forsake you."
HEBREWS 13:5

Technology now exists that allows us to track the location of a particular smartphone. Let's say parents are concerned about their daughter driving alone back to college, in stormy weather, after a visit. Via their phone, the parents can track their daughter's journey until she arrives safely. In case of car trouble, they know her exact location. "I'll be there with you all the way" takes on new meaning in the digital age.

In the Old Testament, that security was expressed another way: "I will never leave you nor forsake you." That was God's promise to the Israelites as they prepared to cross the Jordan River and move into Canaan—and face the Canaanite tribes that occupied their land (Deuteronomy 31:6). God's presence was one of *protection*. But in the New Testament, the same promise of God was applied to *provision*. The writer of Hebrews told his readers not to be covetous but to be content with what they had. Why? Because God would be their provision. He would be with them and never leave them.

Whether you need protection, provision, or something else—you have it in the God who has promised to always be with you.

AUGUST 10
Infinite Goodness

My defense is of God, who saves the upright in heart.
PSALM 7:10

In 1849, Asiatic cholera spread through America. During the outbreak approximately 4,500 people died in St. Louis, 3,000 in New Orleans, and 5,000 in New York City, where many victims were buried in a mass grave on Randall's Island. President Zachary Taylor proclaimed a National Day of Fasting, calling Americans to "humble themselves before His throne, and, while acknowledging past transgressions, ask a continuance of the Divine mercy." He urged them "to acknowledge the Infinite Goodness which has watched over our existence as a nation, and so long crowned us with manifold blessings, and to implore the Almighty in His own good time to stay the destroying hand."

On Friday, August 3, 1849, Americans filed into churches to unite in humility and prayer; and by the end of the month the death toll "dropped suddenly," and the plague abated.

Our world is stained by sin, filled with suffering, and subject to plagues. But there's never a time we can't humble ourselves before God's throne, acknowledge our sins, and ask for a continuance of divine mercy. His all-powerful hand can preserve and protect us, and His infinite wisdom can direct our affairs. His sovereignty is the source of our strength and stability.

AUGUST 11
A Very Present Help

*You know my sitting down and my rising up; You understand
my thought afar off. You comprehend my path and my
lying down, and are acquainted with all my ways.*
PSALM 139:2-3

Grief counselors recommend listening when comforting the
suffering. Listening is a selfless, empathetic act, a way to be
silently present: "You are not alone in your pain; I am here
with you."

God is like the listener—always there, listening to our
thoughts and words, letting us know we are not alone. He
is "our refuge and strength, a very present help in trouble"
(Psalm 46:1). Nowhere in the Bible is God's very presence more
beautifully expressed than in Psalm 139:1-16. When David was
troubled by the adversaries of God who sought to discredit
Him, he poured out his heart to God. In doing so, David
recounted all the ways God was present with him, always ready
to know and understand his thoughts. God was omnipresent—
always and everywhere present—to David and had been from
the moment of his conception in his mother's womb (verses
13-16).

If you find yourself alone today, or in a troubling place,
know that God and His great and precious promises are with
you (2 Peter 1:4).

AUGUST 12
Tribulation Now

We have access by faith into this grace .... And not only that, but we also glory in tribulations.

ROMANS 5:2-3

When the Bible speaks of tribulation, it isn't always talking about the coming Great Tribulation. The English term *tribulation* comes from a Latin word meaning "to press or squeeze." Jesus warned all His followers, "In the world you will have tribulation; but be of good cheer, I have overcome the world" (John 16:33).

We also find this word in Paul's writings. In Romans 5, he tells us that when we are justified by faith, we have: (1) peace with God—verse 1; (2) access to grace—verse 2; (3) assurance of glory—verse 2; (4) and reversal of grief—verses 3-4. Paul wrote, "We also glory in tribulations, knowing that tribulation produces perseverance; and perseverance, character; and character, hope" (verses 3-4).

That doesn't mean we're glad when tribulation comes. It means we're glad for the knowledge that whenever we find ourselves in trouble, God knows how to manage it and redeem the circumstances. Whenever we face troubles, we're in the zone of grace. Trust God and let Him use trouble to produce perseverance, character, and hope in your heart.

AUGUST 13
That Glorious Day

For you yourselves know perfectly that the day of
the Lord so comes as a thief in the night.
1 THESSALONIANS 5:2

When the apostle Paul planted a church in Thessalonica, he had little time to establish the new believers in their faith. According to Acts 17:2, he was driven from town by a persecuting mob after two or three weeks of teaching. But evidently Paul left the Thessalonians with a deep belief in our Lord's return. They were so eager to learn more about the Second Coming that Paul wrote two letters to them—1 and 2 Thessalonians—answering questions and stoking their anticipation for the Lord's soon appearing in the clouds of glory.

Those letters are for us too. They are full of information about the Rapture of the Church, the resurrection of the dead, and the return of Christ.

Imagine how excited those early believers were to receive Paul's letters and soak in his teaching. We, too, should eagerly digest every word in Scripture about our Lord's promised return as we anticipate the moment of His coming for us. How differently we'd live if, like the Thessalonians, our hearts were seized with anticipation for that glorious day!

AUGUST 18

You Are His

What manner of love the Father has bestowed on us,
that we should be called children of God!

1 JOHN 3:1

Stephanie Fast was a homeless child abandoned by her parents after the Korean War. Living in South Korea, she grew up on the streets fighting for survival. One day she seemed to reach her last stretch of life—tired, hungry, sick, and dying she fell into a mountain of trash. A missionary nurse came along and saw her. This nurse was looking for babies to save, not older kids. But when she got up to move, she couldn't—she was stuck—as if a hand was keeping her from leaving. Then the nurse heard a voice that said, "She is mine," so she picked up Stephanie and took her to a Christian orphanage.

Stephanie was adopted by American parents, and today she has dedicated her life to helping orphans and leading them to Christ. God has used her in incredible ways. She says that although she was abandoned in this life, she was never truly alone. God kept her alive because He had a purpose for her.

No matter who has abandoned you or what you have gone through, God has a purpose for your life. He has called you to be His child. Like Stephanie, you can know that no matter who has left you, there is One who has not and never will. You are His.

AUGUST 19
God Sees You

Then she called the name of the Lord who spoke to her, You-Are-the-God-Who-Sees; for she said, "Have I also here seen Him who sees me?"
GENESIS 16:13

Abraham and Sarah became impatient while waiting for God to provide them with a son, so Sarah devised a plan—Abraham would have a child with her maid Hagar, and this would be how God would give them a son. All went according to plan. But once Hagar was expecting a child, Sarah and Hagar's relationship deteriorated rapidly, causing Hagar to flee into the wilderness. It's there in the wilderness that an Angel of the Lord found her and showed her compassion. God came into Hagar's life in a way she had never experienced before, and she entered into a relationship with her Maker that changed her forever.

Sometimes we feel like Hagar did—alone and unwanted in the wilderness—but we are valuable to God. He looks for us and finds us wherever we are. Even when we feel alone or forsaken, God knows where we are, and He promises to never leave us nor forsake us (Deuteronomy 31:6). Our relationship with "the-God-Who-Sees" brings us comfort in the wilderness.

Bless the Lord, you His angels, who excel in strength,
who do His word, heeding the voice of His word.
PSALM 103:20

Think of the number of English surnames that derive from an occupation: Baker, Mason, Butcher, Carpenter, Miller, Smith, and more. The same is true of the name given to spiritual beings created by God. In both Hebrew and Greek, they are called messengers. In English we call them angels, which is the Greek word for messenger (*angelos*) rendered in English (*angel*).

Spiritual angels are divine messengers from God in heaven to us here on earth. Interestingly, the description Paul gave of a messenger (Epaphroditus) from the church in Philippi while he was in prison suggests the role of God's angels to us: "your messenger ... the one who ministered to my need" (Philippians 2:25). That is certainly consistent with the description of angels in Hebrews 1:14: "ministering spirits." The manifestation of angels in our lives can be described like this: We have needs; God cares about our needs; God sends His angels to minister to us, even when we are unaware of their presence.

We should remain thankful and aware of yet another dimension of God's care for us through His ministering messengers we call angels.

AUGUST 21
Immovable

Therefore, my beloved brethren, be steadfast, immovable, always abounding in the work of the Lord, knowing that your labor is not in vain in the Lord.

1 CORINTHIANS 15:58

Paul's letter to the people at Corinth was an exhortation to remain steadfast. The church in Corinth was an undisciplined church, and he was letting them know that even though the culture around them was in flux, their faith in Jesus Christ needed to remain focused and sure. It is true for us today also. How can we remain steadfast in our faith and avoid the pressures of this ever-changing world? By devoting time each day to the study of God's Word.

As we read the Bible and immerse ourselves in God's truth and character, our lives are changed—we become more like Him. God's Word is a powerful litmus test for our souls and actions. As our lives center on God, giving priority to hearing His voice and reading His Word, we become bolder in sharing our faith.

Joshua had the confidence and courage to lead God's people into the Promised Land because he believed in God's promise and presence. We serve the same God who said: "And the Lord, He is the One who goes before you. He will be with you, He will not leave you nor forsake you; do not fear nor be dismayed" (Deuteronomy 31:8).

You can place your steadfast trust in Him.

AUGUST 22
Godly in an Ungodly Age

Beloved, I beg you as sojourners and pilgrims, abstain from fleshly lusts which war against the soul, having your conduct honorable among the Gentiles.

1 PETER 2:11-12

In our modern culture, it seems there are few safe harbors. Danger and temptation lurk on every corner and on millions of Internet websites. Some believe we live in the most dangerous era in history—there is some truth to that. But darkness is nothing new. Even in the first century, the apostle Peter wrote to the first generation of Christians scattered throughout the Mediterranean world, encouraging them to abstain from the dangers by which they were surrounded.

But how? How is it possible to live a spotless life when sin and stain are all around us? In his second letter, Peter picked up that theme and gave the answer: "His divine power has given to us all things that pertain to life and godliness, through the knowledge of Him who called us by glory and virtue" (2 Peter 1:3). Through Christ, we have the ability to manifest virtue, knowledge, self-control, perseverance, godliness, brotherly kindness, and love. Adding these in increasing amounts will lead to us being effective and fruitful followers of Christ (2 Peter 1:5-8).

Don't cower in fear at the darkness. Be the light! In Christ, our faith has "overcome the world" (John 16:33; 1 John 5:4).

AUGUST 23
What Is the Key?

Woe to you lawyers! For you have taken away the key of knowledge. You did not enter in yourselves, and those who were entering in you hindered.

LUKE 11:52

If you search for "the key to" on the "books" page of Amazon.com, over fifty thousand results are returned—books that use "the key to" (or similar words) in their title. In other words, if you discover the key(s) to something—love, photography, algebra, financial success—you have a future as an author! Mentioning "the key" to anything will attract interest.

Jesus mentioned "the key" to something without defining what the key was. After dressing down the Pharisees for their hypocrisy and self-righteousness (Luke 11:39-51), Jesus said they had taken away "the key of knowledge," preventing others from finding knowledge for themselves (verse 52). But what is the key to spiritual knowledge? Jesus didn't say. But since He followed Isaiah's pattern of "woes" (Isaiah 5:8-23) in His words to the Pharisees, we might find a clue to the key in the great prophet's book. Indeed, Isaiah says that the "fear of the Lord" is the key to the treasure of wisdom and knowledge (Isaiah 33:6, NIV). That fits with Jesus' context—the Pharisees gave no evidence of humbly fearing the Lord.

Do you want to discover God's wisdom and knowledge? Live humbly and obediently before Him. Fear (honor) the Lord by keeping His Word (Psalm 111:10).

Rejoice in the Lord always. Again I will say, rejoice!
PHILIPPIANS 4:4

Too often we read the Bible without giving due credence to the humanity of its authors. Yes, the Holy Spirit inspired the human authors, but that inspiration was in the midst of real-life situations in the authors' lives. Looking behind the scenes can pay rich dividends and offer new applications.

Take Paul's letter to the Philippians. It is one of four letters Paul wrote while in prison in Rome, the Prison Epistles: Ephesians, Philippians, Colossians, and Philemon. The first three are relatively the same length (Philemon being only one short chapter), yet Philippians is unique for its focus on joy. Paul mentions joy and rejoicing more than a dozen times in Philippians, but not once in Ephesians and only twice in Colossians. Why was Paul so focused on joy when writing to the Philippians? Perhaps it was partly because of the joy the Philippians had brought him in his imprisonment—gifts to make his time under arrest more comfortable. There is no record of any other church sending similar gifts. The Philippians' gift reminded Paul that, even in hard times, there is joy to be found from the love of others.

If someone brings you joy by serving or loving you, be sure to express your thanks. Letting others know how they have blessed you is an act of true joy.

Honor all people. Love the brotherhood. Fear God. Honor the king.
1 PETER 2:17

How do you respond when the person over you in some capacity—supervisor, employer, political official—is a person with whom you have nothing in common spiritually or culturally? Sometimes it's easy to manifest one's loss of respect or one's disagreement in ways that are not helpful.

Joseph is a good example to consider. After being sold into slavery by his brothers, he eventually rose to a position of prominence in Egypt as the chief steward of Potiphar, a powerful Egyptian official. As a Hebrew descendant of Abraham, Joseph had a worldview markedly different from his pagan employer. And yet he served his employer with such respect that he was entrusted with all of Potiphar's affairs. The only thing Potiphar did was show up at mealtimes—Joseph handled everything else (Genesis 39:6). Joseph is a good example of Peter's words: "Honor all people." Peter used a Greek word that looks at humanity ("people") as a whole. Humanity deserves to be honored, if not always in the same way. Even when we disagree, people deserve honor as human beings.

The next time you find yourself disagreeing with someone—a spouse, a friend, a boss, a president—remember Peter's words: "Honor all people." Everyone bears God's image, regardless of how tarnished you think it may be (Genesis 1:26-27).

Peace I leave with you, My peace I give to you;
not as the world gives do I give to you.
JOHN 14:27

Our world is in constant search for peace—peace with other nations, peace with our neighbors and friends, and peace with our self. But there is one peace that is eternal and can only be granted by our Heavenly Father—it is the peace of God.

The word "peace" occurs in 369 verses in the Bible. When the disciples were caught in a storm and overwhelmed by fear, Jesus said, "Peace, be still!" (Mark 4:39) When the sick woman touched Jesus' garment and was healed, He told her to "go in peace" (Mark 5:34). Jesus came to earth to give us peace (John 14:27). When Jesus appeared in the Upper Room after His resurrection, His followers were afraid, and He told them, "Peace be with you" (John 20:19).

If you are caught in the storm of life, God's peace is the only true power that can calm the waves. Finding worldly peace is temporary but resting in His peace is everlasting. His peace is indestructible. If you are facing turmoil, ask the Lord for His heavenly peace—it surpasses anything we could understand!

Remind the people to be … peaceable and considerate,
and always to be gentle toward everyone.
TITUS 3:1-2, NIV

Alton and Delois Loveless traveled to an island to help in a
Vacation Bible School, and when local workers learned the
couple's anniversary would occur that week they planned a
surprise party. In one of the sessions, the children and workers
gathered around a huge cake with thin sugar icing. Alton and
Delois were told to cut the cake and feed a piece to each other.
As Alton shoved the cake into his wife's mouth, her eyes were
tightly closed, and she had an unpleasant look on her face.
Later he asked her about it. "Didn't you see the ants and bugs
all over the cake and icing?" she replied. "I knew the expense
and the work those dear people had gone to for us, so I was not
going to hurt their feelings for the world. Because of that I was
willing to eat it ants and all."[15]

Being considerate means working hard to avoid hurting the
feelings of others. Love "does not behave rudely" (1 Corinthians
13:5). Though rudeness is in style now, true strength is wrapped
in gentleness, kindness, and consideration.

[15] Altonloveless.blogspot.com/2007/08/she-ate-it-ants-and-all.html

Believe on the Lord Jesus Christ, and you will be saved.
ACTS 16:31

In her book, *Let's Be Friends*, Elizabeth Hoagland told of the time her pastor, Bob Russell, went to hear the great New Testament scholar Dr. Lewis Foster preach. Bob took his five-year-old son with him. Dr. Foster had graduated from Harvard and had served on the translation team for the New International Version Study Bible, and his message was deep, yet stated simply. Bob drunk in Dr. Foster's sermon with joy, but he wasn't prepared for what Rusty, his son, later said. The five-year-old, with typical childlike honesty, suggested his dad try preaching like Dr. Foster because, he said, he could understand him.

Back home, Bob sat down and wrote out the Gospel message in one-syllable words: "God made man and loved him. Man sinned and fell from God's grace. But God, in His great love, sent His Son to die in our place, and then He raised Him from the dead. Now if we put our faith in Him, He will cleanse our sins and give us life."

Nothing is deeper than simplicity, and even the depths of theological truth can be taught to children of all ages. God has made His message understandable.

Why are you angry? And why has your countenance fallen?
GENESIS 4:6

Rage rooms have opened in cities around the world. The first one opened in Japan around 2008, and since then they've popped up in cities everywhere. These are places where for a fee people can go to smash things, throw things, break things, and release their stress. In New York City, a special $95 couples package is available with two buckets of dishes and two electronic items a couple can smash.

Maybe there's a better way to do the needed maintenance on your anger management. Here are some suggestions.

Confess your anger to God and ask Him to show you the roots of your rage. Apologize to those who have been on the receiving end of your anger. Read all you can on the subject of anger management because the more you learn about your emotions, the more likely you'll be able to manage them wisely. Locate and memorize a handful of Bible verses on anger and quote them to yourself often. Finally, know when to get help. God can lead you to someone gifted with wisdom who can help you mature in your reactions to life.

Begin today; stop the madness and learn the power of spiritual patience and divine mercy.

SEPTEMBER 10
What Love Covers

This is a faithful saying and worthy of all acceptance, that Christ Jesus came into the world to save sinners, of whom I am chief.

1 TIMOTHY 1:15

The phrase "Damascene experience" is used in modern contexts to describe a sudden awakening, a moment of insight leading to a reversal of priorities and values, or a shock to one's worldview. Its basis, of course, is in the apostle Paul's encounter with the resurrected Christ on the road to Damascus where he intended to persecute the followers of Jesus.

Two great injustices—in the legal sense of the word—occur in the New Testament. First, the perfectly innocent Jesus of Nazareth was put to death, while second, the perfectly guilty Saul of Tarsus was forgiven and set free. We know why Jesus died—to take away the sins of the world (John 1:29). But why was Paul forgiven and set free from his guilt? In order that he might experience first-hand what God wanted him to proclaim to the Gentile world: the love and grace of God. Saul (later Paul) was guilty of persecuting innocent Christians, yet God's love covered all his sins.

"Love covers all sins" (Proverbs 10:12)—even all of yours. Be secure today in God's love.

SEPTEMBER 11
His Mercy Endures Forever

Oh, give thanks to the Lord, for He is good! For His mercy endures forever.
PSALM 136:1

Some people in our culture view God strictly as a judge. They think He's out to get them. Yes, God is holy, and He judges sin. But God is also merciful—the Gospel is evidence of this. Whatever God does—whether it's a display of power or justice, severity or wrath—is a display of His mercy. In Psalm 136 the author listed God's works on Israel's behalf followed by the refrain, "For His mercy endures forever." Their deliverance from Egypt, the striking down of evil kings, and the land He gave them were all evidences of God's mercy on His people.

God demonstrates the same mercy to us. He provides us with "the sun to rule by day … the moon and stars to rule by night," and He "gives food to all flesh" (Psalm 136:8-9, 25). His mercies are all around us, daily reminders of His love and care for us. The psalmist was led to praise as he reflected on God's mercy to the people of Israel, and God's mercy leads us to praise Him too. As we reflect on what God has done for us, we can say with the psalmist, "Oh, give thanks to the God of heaven! For His mercy endures forever" (verse 26).

SEPTEMBER 12
Imitate Me

But as He who called you is holy, you also be holy in all your conduct, because it is written, "Be holy, for I am holy."
1 PETER 1:15-16

Children learn by imitating the actions—good and bad—of those around them. Often they imitate their parents, which can lead to an embarrassing moment for the parent, particularly when a child repeats a phrase that contains words they shouldn't say.

In 1 Peter 1:15 God tells us to imitate Him, to be holy because He is holy. Holiness is the complete absence of any taint of evil. God is holy in all of His being, His words and ways. He desires us to be the same. However, when we look at our life in light of God's holiness, the enormity and reality of our sin embarrasses us.

We will not be perfectly holy while we are here on earth, but God's purpose for us is that we cultivate holiness in our life. How do we cultivate holiness? As we face challenges and choices each day, we need to pray for God to help us do the right thing, the "holy" thing, instead of the thing which might be more beneficial or comfortable for us.

I planted, Apollos watered, but God gave the increase.
1 CORINTHIANS 3:6

The legendary basketball coach John Wooden wrote, "Andre McCarter was not the best guard I ever coached. Nor was Pete Trgovich. However, together they were probably the best defensive pair of guards I ever had. Each increased the effectiveness of the other .... Andre and Pete had the right chemistry." He went on to say, "I was always looking for a great player. But even more I was looking for the ... combination of players, who could make the team great."

This is also true in marriage and in ministry.

In a marriage, each partner has strengths and weaknesses, but as they learn to work together they discover that the impact of their influence is greater than the sum of the parts. Each draws effectiveness from the other, combining strengths and minimizing weaknesses. This usually doesn't happen automatically. As in basketball, it takes lots of practice.

In your local church, the same is true. When you're on a ministry team of some sort, each should make the other stronger. In the process, God adds His blessings and gives the increase. Learn to be a team player wherever you are.

*To this end I strenuously contend with all the
energy Christ so powerfully works in me.*
COLOSSIANS 1:29, NIV

John Wanamaker was a Philadelphia businessman who built the largest department store in the world, yet his business enterprise was secondary to his running a Sunday School and establishing a church in the same city. His wealth allowed him to finance large endeavors of Christian ministry, including the work of evangelist D. L. Moody, and Wanamaker was always concerned about winning people to Christ.

Wanamaker often spoke on the subject of success, and he said, "Three-quarters of all work is drudgery unless we love it and keep cheerful .... Every man is at his best when he adds enthusiasm to whatever he honestly believes in. Both power and progress will then enter into his undertakings."

When we awaken each morning, our eyes open to a new set of assignments from God. Whether we're polishing the furniture or ruling a nation, we're simply to do what God has appointed for us. But we're to do it with cheerfulness and enthusiasm, strenuously working with all the energy Christ so powerfully works in us.

Let's serve the Lord with gladness!

SEPTEMBER 23
A Royal Problem

*Do not rejoice when your enemy falls, and do not let your
heart be glad when he stumbles …. Love does not envy.*
PROVERBS 24:17; 1 CORINTHIANS 13:4

The tabloids had a field day claiming Kate Middleton and
Meghan Markle were so jealous of each other it affected the
relationship between their husbands—the brothers William
and Harry. Evidently the two British royal couples were moving
farther away from each other and putting distance between
themselves because Meghan's glamorous fame overshadowed
Kate. Well, don't believe what you read in the tabloids. Who
knows what happens behind palace walls? But we do know
from our own experience how easily the attitudes of envy
and jealousy can affect our relationships. They can cause
breakdowns between family members, church members,
coworkers, or classmates. They can create distance between us.

Our natural human emotions are envy and jealousy, and
that's a royal problem. Our supernatural biblical emotions
rejoice at the achievements of others. If you feel the pinch of
jealous frustration, confess it to the Lord as sin and remember
this: When we possess the true Spirit-given love of Jesus, we're
happy for the success of another.

Then last of all he sent his son.
MATTHEW 21:37

Prior to His crucifixion, Jesus used parables to debate the religious leaders in the temple. In one, He compared the nation of Israel to a vineyard under the control of tenants who rejected those sent by the owner to collect his share of the grapes. The owner sent messenger after messenger, but the tenants beat them, stoned them, and killed them. Finally he sent his own son. But the wicked tenants threw him out of the vineyard and killed him.

The meaning of the parable is clear. Throughout the Old Testament, the Lord sent one messenger after another to His people. He sent leaders like Moses and David, and prophets like Isaiah, Jeremiah, and Ezekiel. Last of all, God sent His Son.

The Lord still goes to great lengths to reach us today. Perhaps the Lord has been sending you one message after another. You had a pricking of your conscience. You heard a snippet of a sermon on television. Your friend invited you to church. You had a close escape from a car wreck. Don't be like the wicked tenants. Respond to Him and give your life wholeheartedly to Jesus Christ.

SEPTEMBER 25
Comedy of Errors

Counsel is mine, and sound wisdom; I am understanding, I have strength.
PROVERBS 8:14

In 2018, a man in Colorado planned to rob a store, but he drew attention to himself by pacing on the sidewalk, gathering his courage. Then he entered the store and pulled a gun from his clothes—it was a BB gun—but he lost his grip and sent it tumbling behind the counter where the clerk picked it up. The man then ran from the store, but his pants, once held up with his BB gun in the waistband, fell around his legs.

It's amazing how our foolish deeds start multiplying on us.

It's also amazing how our wise deeds multiply. Our actions flow from values and convictions, and our wisdom comes from God. He says, "Counsel is mine, and sound wisdom; I am understanding, I have strength."

Life is confusing for us, but we don't have to bungle our way through it. Ask God for wisdom for each day and study the counsel of His Word. The fruit of righteousness abounds with each passing year; instead of a comedy of errors, our life becomes a channel of blessing.

OCTOBER 6
The Object of Jealousy

For you shall worship no other god, for the Lord,
whose name is Jealous, is a jealous God.
EXODUS 34:14

Sometimes reading the Bible raises questions. For instance, we are warned in Scripture to avoid jealousy and envy—it is "rottenness to the bones" (Proverbs 14:30)—and yet one of God's names in the Old Testament is "Jealous"—for He is "a jealous God" (Exodus 34:14). Why is jealousy an attribute for God but a sin for us?

Because of the motivation. God is not jealous for us because He envies something we have that He doesn't have. Instead, think of "jealous" as "zealous"—God loves us so much that He is zealous for us to worship Him alone, to live in close communion with Him. God is jealous for us because He knows we will benefit from our devotion to Him. On the other hand, when we are jealous, it is for selfish reasons. We want something for our own pleasure that another person has. God's jealousy is others-centered; human jealousy is self-centered.

If you find yourself being jealous, ask yourself, Who is the object of my feelings? Do I want the best for the other person or the best for myself?

OCTOBER 7
"But I Did Not"

But I did not do so, because of the fear of God.
NEHEMIAH 5:15

When Nehemiah became governor of the land of Judah, he and his family refused the common practice of having their meals provided from government funds. While there may have been nothing wrong with taxpayer-funded food for the nation's leader, former governors had abused the practice. Their excessive lifestyles had burdened the people, and Nehemiah wanted to avoid even the appearance of wrongdoing. So he paid his own way because he feared God and wanted to protect his integrity for God's sake.

Are there areas of your life in which you should draw some lines, erect some barriers, build some fences, and establish some standards? Any habits you should change? Our society has no established moral code, and the standards keep changing. We must not let the world keep rubbing out the lines we draw for ourselves. The Bible calls us to personal holiness, and our integrity comes from the standards we adopt.

"Don't let the world around you squeeze you into its own mould, but let God re-mould your minds from within" (Romans 12:2, PHILLIPS).

OCTOBER 12
Stand Out for Christ

*But put on the Lord Jesus Christ, and make no
provision for the flesh, to fulfill its lusts.*
ROMANS 13:14

In the Old Testament, a Nazarite (from the Hebrew "to vow")
was a person who took a vow of separation unto the Lord—
temporarily or permanently. Of the latter category, there were
only three named: Samson, Samuel, and John the Baptist. It
meant being different in many ways—a life wholly dedicated
to God.

When John the Baptist's parents were told by the angel
Gabriel that their son would be the forerunner of the Messiah,
they knew it meant releasing their son unto God's calling.
When John appeared on the scene as an adult, announcing the
coming of Jesus, he was indeed different: dressed in garments
made of camel hair and a leather belt, eating locusts and wild
honey. By his appearance first, then his words, John stood out
in Judea as he proclaimed Jesus.

We are not called to put on garments made of camel
hair, but we are called to put on Jesus Christ (Romans 13:14;
Galatians 3:27). It is Christ in us that will cause us to be
different in this world.

Your word I have hidden in my heart, that I might not sin against You.
PSALM 119:11

There are around one thousand quotes, references, and allusions to the Old Testament in the New Testament. When New Testament writers wrote their Gospels and letters, they might have had Old Testament scrolls with which to check their quotations and references. But what about when Jesus and the apostles quoted the Old Testament "on the fly"—during the course of their ministry? In those cases, they were quoting from memory, not from a scroll. They took the Old Covenant admonition seriously to know God's Word by heart.

Such was the case when Jesus responded to Satan's three temptations in the wilderness—He quoted three verses from Deuteronomy from memory (Matthew 4:1-11). If we are going to defeat Satan's lies and temptations with the truth of God, we must store up the Word of God in our heart like the psalmist— "that [we] might not sin against [God]."

While in the midst of temptation is not the time to begin your search for Scriptures. Begin today to be prepared—to commit God's Word to memory. (Psalm 119:11 is a good place to begin.)

OCTOBER 30
Maze Daze

My eyes flow and do not cease, without interruption,
till the Lord from heaven looks down and sees.
LAMENTATIONS 3:49-50

Cool Patch Pumpkins in Dixon, California, has the largest corn maze in the world—about sixty acres of winding paths between towering stalks of corn. Every year during maze season authorities brace for 911 calls. After wandering for hours, visitors panic. "I don't know what to do anymore," one caller said. "We've been in here like four hours." Another said, "We're stuck, and they close at 10. We're very worried, and we can't find a way out."

What a parable of life! We all encounter twists and turns, dead ends and puzzling circumstances. But if you took a helicopter over the maze, you would see a distinct route. In fact, the maze often spells out words when viewed from above. The maze is actually amazing.

If you feel lost in your circumstances, remember that God is looking down from above and it all makes perfect sense to Him. His handwriting has spelled out a perfect plan for you. Even when we don't understand our circumstances, we can be confident in God's grace and guidance.

Blessed be the Lord, who has given rest to His people Israel, according to all that He promised. There has not failed one word of all His good promise.

1 KINGS 8:56

King Solomon prayed one of the Bible's longest prayers when he dedicated the temple in Jerusalem in 1 Kings 8, and the occasion was a highwater mark in Jewish history. The glory of God descended and a cloud filled the temple. Solomon, overwhelmed, knelt before the Lord, raised his hands toward heaven, and led his people in a deeply meaningful prayer of dedication. Then, lifting himself to his feet, he addressed his people and praised God with thanksgiving. "There has not failed one word of all His good promise," he said.

There were times when Solomon failed—and times when the Jewish people failed. The priests and prophets were subject to failure, and sometimes the entire nation failed. But God cannot fail, will not fail, and His promises will never falter. His faithfulness doesn't depend on our perfection; it's rooted in His perfect faithfulness, for there is no shadow of turning with Him.

If you're worried about your faults and failures, confess them to God and turn your eyes back to Christ's great faithfulness, mercy, and love.

NOVEMBER

NOVEMBER 1
A Constant Invitation

*And he arose and came to his father. But when he was still
a great way off, his father saw him and had compassion,
and ran and fell on his neck and kissed him.*
LUKE 15:20

The prodigal son was still a far way off. There was no guarantee
of his repentance. Perhaps he was returning to demand more
money. Yet, in this parable, we see the father rushing toward his
son, as soon as he is within sight.

Throughout the Gospels, Jesus is compassionate. His words
and power transform and heal one person at a time. Even in
His rage and harsh words to the Pharisees and Sadducees, He
is motivated by a heart broken over their dead faith and the
heavy burdens they are inflicting on others.

Jesus proclaims His desire that no one should perish.
As Christians, we not only receive Christ's compassion for
ourselves, but we also get to share it with the world through
our actions and words, inviting others to experience Christ for
themselves. Who will you show compassion to today?

NOVEMBER 30
A Merry Heart

A merry heart does good, like medicine, but a broken spirit dries the bones.
PROVERBS 17:22

A lot of books have been written for high school students preparing them for the ups and downs of living with college roommates. One is called *52 Ways to Get Along With Your College Roommate*. Other titles include: *The Roommate Book*; *The College Roommate From Hell: Skills and Strategies for Surviving With a Problem Roommate*; and *My Roommate Is Driving Me Crazy!*

It isn't easy to live with another person. Whether in a dormitory, in barracks, or in a home, it takes God's grace to live happily and harmoniously. How vital to stay positive and cultivate a merry heart! The Bible says:

- "A merry heart makes a cheerful countenance" (Proverbs 15:13).

- "A merry heart has a continual feast" (Proverbs 15:15).

- "Go, eat your bread with joy, and drink your wine with a merry heart; for God has already accepted your works" (Ecclesiastes 9:7).

May God give us all a merry heart that will be like an elixir for those with whom we live!

DECEMBER

DECEMBER 1
A Gift Fit for a King

*The name of the first [river] is Pishon; it is the one which skirts the whole
land of Havilah, where there is gold. And the gold of that land is good.*
GENESIS 2:11-12

The most timeless store of value in history has been gold. It is
beautiful, durable, malleable, conductive, and does not tarnish.
It has been the precious metal of choice for kings and rulers
through the ages. Gold is the first metal mentioned in the Bible,
suggesting its timeless value (Genesis 2:11-12). In the numerous
places where the three most precious metals are mentioned in
Scripture—gold, silver, and bronze—gold is usually mentioned
first.

Solomon covered the inside of the temple in Jerusalem with
gold—suitable for the dwelling place of God. It is no surprise,
then, that when the Magi came to worship the "King of the
Jews," they brought gold as a gift (Matthew 2:2, 11). As the most
timeless store of value in the world, gold is the right gift for the
One who transcends time—the eternal Son of God.

What gift of gold can we give that is fit for our King?
Our timeless devotion to Him. Let your love for Christ be as
timeless as gold—live in anticipation of the day when you see
Him face to face.

DECEMBER 6
Practicing His Presence

Behold, the virgin shall conceive and bear a Son,
and shall call His name Immanuel.
ISAIAH 7:14

On March 23, 1930, missionary Frank Laubach began a life-long experiment of practicing the presence of God. He wrote in his journal: "Can we have that contact with God all the time? All the time awake, fall asleep in His arms, and awaken in His presence, can we attain that? Can we do His will all the time? Can we think His thoughts all the time?" He wrote, "I choose to make the rest of my life an experiment in answering this question." As he cultivated this habit, it transformed him. He later wrote, "Things which I did with a strain before, I now do easily and with no effort whatever. I worry about nothing and lose no sleep …. Even the mirror reveals a new light in my eyes."

We can enjoy God's continual presence because the name *Immanuel* means "God with us." His prophetically-given name indicates the pouring out of God's personal presence, like a waterfall, descending from highest heaven to lowest earth, giving us access to the flood of His nearness.

Live consciously in His presence today! Think of Him. Listen to Him. Talk to Him. Remind yourself of His closeness. The One called Immanuel said, "I am with you always" (Matthew 28:20).

DECEMBER 7
Pointing the Way

And when Jesus came to the place, He looked up and saw him,
and said to him, "Zacchaeus, make haste and come down,
for today I must stay at your house."
LUKE 19:5

If you encountered someone who was lost and needed help finding the way, would you offer that person a maze instead of a roadmap? Of course not! Most of us would give detailed directions. We might draw a map. We might even offer to personally escort them to their destination.

While Zacchaeus was in the tree, Jesus discerned his lost condition and need for direction in his life. So He stopped what He was doing to talk with Zacchaeus and took the time to personally show him the way.

To always be ready and willing to share our faith means we must first be aware that there are those around us who are lost. We must look for those who are wandering aimlessly through life and offer to help them find their way, even before we're asked.

To make ourselves available to the lost may interrupt our schedule and take us out of our way. But in doing so, we tread the path already mapped out by Christ, our Savior and our Lord, who came to seek and save the lost.

DECEMBER 8
Blessed December

Let not your heart be troubled.
JOHN 14:1

Wouldn't it be wonderful if we could suspend all wars for the month of December in honor of Christ's birth? We've read about the amazing Christmas Eve truce of World War I when German and Allied soldiers sang carols, exchanged gifts, and played soccer on the battlefields of Flanders. Why can't the armies of the world declare December a month of peace? What if no diseases struck during December? No deaths occurred? No funerals were necessary?

We live in a deadly, disease-ridden, war-weary world, and there's no cessation of trouble. But the Lord Jesus Christ can give *inner* peace, and He can provide assurance of *eternal* peace. In one of His greatest promises, He said, "Peace I leave with you, My peace I give to you; not as the world gives do I give to you. Let not your heart be troubled, neither let it be afraid" (John 14:27).

How personal! Notice the phrases: ... *with you* ... *to you* ... *to you* ... *your heart*.

We don't know how to suspend war or wickedness, but as Christians we walk with the Lord and experience His peace every day of December and beyond.

The Hopes and Fears

Grant us that we ... might serve Him without fear, in holiness and righteousness before Him all the days of our life.
LUKE 1:74-75

When Phillips Brooks wrote the carol, "O Little Town of Bethlehem," he coined a phrase that sums up our emotions about Christmas: "The hopes and fears of all the years are met in thee tonight." It's too beautiful a line to alter, but let's remember that the hope of Jesus overcame the fears of all the years. Because of Jesus we can release our fears, anxieties, apprehensions, and nervous sorrows.

When you read through Luke's Gospel, beginning with the Nativity, you keep running into the phrase, "Do not be afraid." The angel said that to Zacharias in Luke 1:13, to Mary in Luke 1:30, and to the shepherds in Luke 2:10. Jesus later told Simon Peter in Luke 5:10: "Do not be afraid." And He told a worried father named Jairus, "Do not be afraid; only believe" (Luke 8:50).

One of the most powerful prayers is found in Luke 1:76-79, when Zacharias prayed that God would enable us to serve Him without fear all the days of our life. Whatever is bothering you today, don't be afraid. Serve the Lord without fear, in holiness and righteousness, all the days of your life.

DECEMBER 10
The Incense of Worship

And the Lord said to Moses: "Take sweet spices, stacte and onycha and galbanum, and pure frankincense with these sweet spices; there shall be equal amounts of each. You shall make of these an incense."
EXODUS 30:34-35

For thousands of years, the tree *arbor thurifera*, growing in the Arabian Peninsula and Lebanon, has been tapped for its resin. The bark was cut, and exuding resin was allowed to dry as nodules, or "tears." When hardened, the resin, called frankincense, was ground into a fine powder. When subjected to a flame, it gave off a sweet and powerful aroma—an incense used in the worship of God in the tabernacle and temple. ("Frankincense" derives from the old French *franc encens*, meaning "highest-quality incense.")

When the Magi journeyed to Bethlehem and saw the baby Jesus, they "fell down and worshiped Him," presenting frankincense—the most noble incense of worship—as one of their gifts (Matthew 2:11). Paul refers to the life of the Christian as a living sacrifice, a reasonable service of worship (Romans 12:1). That service becomes a wonderful aroma—the incense of worshipful service—in our life (Philippians 4:18).

What gift of frankincense can we give to Christ this Christmas? The highest quality incense of service to Him and to others is—the aroma of Christ in us.

For unto us a Child is born, unto us a Son is given; and the government will
be upon His shoulder. And His name will be called Wonderful, Counselor.
ISAIAH 9:6

As Christmas approaches, we turn our attention to the One
who came to deliver us from sin forever. Isaiah 9:6 tells us that
He was *born*—speaking of His humanity, but it also says that
He was *given*—reminding us that He is deity.

In calling Jesus the Wonderful Counselor, Isaiah is
reminding us that we can come to Him for the same kind of
wisdom a loyal subject would seek from a ruling king.

When we enter into His courts, we recognize that we
are the subjects of a Great Ruler who sees everything in His
kingdom and knows how to best rule over it all. We can bring
our questions and concerns to Him and seek His divine and
eternal guidance with confidence that He will direct us in the
very best way.

When we seek the Lord's royal wisdom and guidance, we
participate with Him in changing our hearts and our emotions.
When we consult with Him and allow Him to reign as our
Wonderful Counselor, we gain an inside track to joyful and
abundant living in Him.

DECEMBER 12
Myrrh

And Nicodemus, who at first came to Jesus by night, also came, bringing a mixture of myrrh and aloes, about a hundred pounds.
JOHN 19:39

Like frankincense, myrrh was a resin extracted from a host of small, thorny trees in the Middle East. The resin was valued as a perfume, as incense, and also as medicine. It was traded as a valuable spice in the Old Testament (Genesis 37:25) and as an ingredient in sacred anointing oil (Exodus 30:23-25).

So, when the Magi came to present their gifts to the Christ-Child, why did they include myrrh (Matthew 2:11)? As a valuable commodity, it represented a sacrifice on the Magi's part. But there was a deeper meaning foreshadowed in their gift—its medicinal use and perfuming use suggested the coming death of the King of the Jews. Indeed, when Jesus hung on the cross He was given "wine mingled with myrrh to drink" (Mark 15:23). And when He was entombed, myrrh was one of the aromatic spices used when His body was wrapped in graveclothes (John 19:39).

What myrrh-like gift can we give to Christ this Christmas? We can live the reality of having died with Christ and been raised to new life in Him.

DECEMBER 13
Say "Yes"

Then Mary said [to the angel], "Behold the maidservant of the Lord! Let it be to me according to your word." And the angel departed from her.
LUKE 1:38

A certain grocery store encourages people to bring their own shopping bags by having them fill out a ticket for a drawing with their name and phone number (if they spend more than $25 in the store). If they win the weekly drawing, they get $25 of free groceries. People have filled out the ticket scores of times without winning, but they dutifully continue. Why? Because they know who will never win: *those who don't say "Yes."*

Filling out a ticket for free groceries is a bit of an act of faith—but not like biblical faith. The grocery store doesn't promise your faith will be rewarded, but God does: "He is a rewarder of those who" have faith in Him (Hebrews 11:6). Saying "Yes" to God is an act of faith that brings blessing and reward. Did Mary the mother of Jesus have the choice to say "No" to God? Humanly, it seems she did. But she chose to believe God's messenger and say "Yes." And we are blessed because she did.

Let your default answer to God be "Yes"—and trust Him to reward your faith in His way (2 Corinthians 1:20).

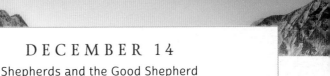

The Lord is my shepherd; I shall not want.

PSALM 23:1

The story is told of a graduate of a top-tier, Ivy League college who took a vocational placement test. He was sure he would find himself suited for being a banker, doctor, lawyer, or executive of a huge corporation. When he read the results, to his embarrassed surprise, the test indicated he was best suited to be a shepherd.

A few thousand years earlier that could have been a badge of honor—it was normal for kings, priests, and other leaders to be referred to as shepherds. God certainly referred to the leaders of Israel that way (Ezekiel 34). But due to their failure to shepherd God's people, He told them He Himself would become their Shepherd. How fitting, therefore, that the angels of heaven chose humble, Bethlehem shepherds as the recipients of the announcement of God's incarnation on earth—the incarnation of the One who would become the Good Shepherd (John 10:1-21).

Psalm 23 is a wonderful Christmas meditation—the image of the Lord as Shepherd of His sheep. If you belong to His flock, then He is leading and caring for you.

The Lord has made known His salvation; His righteousness
He has revealed in the sight of the nations.

PSALM 98:2

Hymn lyrics and tunes stay with us when almost everything else fades. How many of us know of elderly friends, parents, or spouses with memory loss? Some of these senior saints no longer recognize anything except for the words or music of some great hymn, one they absorbed over the course of a lifetime, one that settled into the deepest spheres of their souls. Historian Ernest Edwin Ryden said, "The memory of a single hymn learned in childhood has often proved decisive in the spiritual crises of later years."

That's especially true for our Christmas carols, because they're deeply intertwined with our annual celebration of the greatest Gift humanity has ever received. Music brings the celebration in our heart into fruition in our very being. It brings the joy of the angels into our life.

Perhaps this season you'll be in a public spot when you hear a Christmas carol playing in the background. Who knows? It might be a good opportunity to look at someone nearby and, with a smile, say, "They're singing about my Savior."

DECEMBER 16
Living by Faith

But while [Joseph] thought about these things, behold, an angel
of the Lord appeared to him in a dream, saying, "Joseph, son
of David, do not be afraid to take to you Mary your wife,
for that which is conceived in her is of the Holy Spirit."

MATTHEW 1:20

We would love to know more about the personal lives of
biblical characters. Take Joseph, for instance—the earthly
father of the Son of God.

How spiritually mature was Joseph? Was he a faithful
Jew—a worshiper of the God of Israel? It appears he was,
given his response to the very unusual situation he was in. His
betrothed, Mary, was pregnant, and his first response was to
divorce her respectfully (Matthew 1:19). But the greater test
came when an angel from God appeared to him in a dream and
counseled him to stay with Mary, to marry her, and to become
the father of her child. Joseph "did as the angel of the Lord
commanded" (Matthew 1:24). Joseph was a living example of
walking by faith, not by sight.

Submitting to God by faith is the ultimate test of
faithfulness. Like Joseph, "do not be afraid" to take God at
His Word.

*Then the angel said to [the shepherds], "Do not be afraid, for behold,
I bring you good tidings of great joy which will be to all people."*
LUKE 2:10

Christmas can be the hardest time of the year. In fact, some
people fear the Christmas season. Perhaps it's the first
Christmas after the death of a loved one. Maybe there are
financial pressures made worse by Christmas bills. If you are
single and without friends or family nearby, Christmas can be a
lonely time.

There was fear at the very first Christmas. Zacharias and
Elizabeth feared never having a child (Luke 1:13). Mary feared
the future and becoming a new bride (Luke 1:30). And the
shepherds in the Bethlehem field feared an encounter with the
supernatural (Luke 2:10). The Christmas message to them is the
same message to us: "Fear not. This is a season of good news and
great joy! A Savior has been born who is Christ, the Lord of all."
There is no fearful circumstance that cannot be defused by the
reality of the Christmas presence of Christ and His Spirit.

Whatever your circumstances this Christmas, let joy and
celebration be your theme. Trust that the God of the first
Christmas is the God of your Christmas as well.

DECEMBER 22

A Proactive Pardon

The next day John saw Jesus coming toward him, and said, "Behold!
The Lamb of God who takes away the sin of the world!"
JOHN 1:29

Article II, Section 2, of the United States Constitution gives
the American President power to pardon those guilty of
breaking federal laws. (States can pardon violators of state
laws.) Usually, requests for presidential pardons are addressed
to the President himself by the person seeking the pardon.
Alternatively, the President can issue a pardon even if one has
not been requested. Acceptance of a pardon is a tacit admission
of guilt—and in such cases, sometimes a presidential pardon is
refused when the recipient doesn't agree to the assumption of
guilt.

In humanity's case, we did not have to request a pardon
from God for our sins. God took it upon Himself to send a
Savior to set sin-scarred humanity free from the guilt of sin.
Jesus said, "[God] has sent Me to ... proclaim liberty to the
captives" (Luke 4:18). The Bible is clear that "all have sinned
and fall short of the glory of God" (Romans 3:23). We know we
need a Savior from sin.

Thank God this Christmas that He sent a Savior to pardon
and save us from all our sins.

DECEMBER 23
Bowing in Humility

And when [the Magi] had come into the house, they saw the young
Child with Mary His mother, and fell down and worshiped Him.
And when they had opened their treasures, they presented gifts
to Him: gold, frankincense, and myrrh.
MATTHEW 2:11

The Japanese people are the most willing to demonstrate
humility in public—by bowing. There are multiple degrees of
bowing—from a slight bow when greeting others to a ninety-
degree, right-angle bow from the waist, held for an appropriate
length of time, when sincere humility or apology is called for.
In extreme cases, a bow from a kneeling position is executed.

Kneeling, even prostrating oneself, is a typical act of
humility. It's the kind of worshipful humility demonstrated by
the Magi when they entered the place where the Christ-Child
lay: "They ... fell down and worshiped Him" before presenting
their gifts to Him. These were important men in their Persian
culture, making their obeisance toward the Child all the more
meaningful. Humility is the sign of our recognition of our
place in God's world.

How might we humble ourselves before Christ this
Christmas? By bowing before Him—spiritually, even
physically—as a demonstration of our recognition of His
Lordship in our life.

All Scripture is given by inspiration of God, and is profitable for doctrine,
for reproof, for correction, for instruction in righteousness.
2 TIMOTHY 3:16

The Babylonians did it and so did the Romans; medieval knights made it a practice as well. New Year's resolutions or promises have been around for centuries—and they are certainly popular today. Polls in recent decades indicate almost as many as half of Americans resolve to "do better" at the beginning of each new year.

No harm in making resolutions, of course. But some may be more important than others—like the resolution to be faithful daily in reading God's Word. After all, the Word of God has the power to teach us, reprove us, correct us, and instruct us in godly living (2 Timothy 3:16). Such power would cover a multitude of things we might make resolutions to change! Scripture can also reveal the "thoughts and intents of the heart" (Hebrews 4:12)—the obstacles in our path that keep us from achieving what we know God wants us to be. The surest way to follow Christ into the new year is to read His Word daily.

As 2020 draws to a close, resolve to read and meditate upon God's Word every day of 2021.

DECEMBER 31
A New Day, a New Hope

For surely there is a hereafter, and your hope will not be cut off.
PROVERBS 23:18

In his song "1999," the late superstar Prince sang, "Life is just a party and parties weren't meant to last." As we know, Prince's party didn't last. He died of a drug overdose in 2016 at age 57. Tonight millions of people will be partying as the old year draws to a close. The beginning of a new year is certainly worth celebrating, but it's also a time to remind ourselves that life isn't simply a party—it's a calling and commission from God. The brevity of life only reinforces the need for each day to be dedicated to knowing and doing the will of God.

Compare Prince's song to this old English hymn by Emily Elliott:

> *Every day He sends us*
> *He Himself prepares;*
> *He Himself attends us*
> *Through its joys and cares;*
> *His true love beseeching,*
> *Let us, then, draw near;*
> *Seeking guidance, teaching,*
> *For the opening year.*